Getting
a Grip
on Your
Money

William C. Wood
Professor of Economics

**A Plain & Simple
Christian Guide to**

Managing Personal
Finances

Eliminating Debt

Spending, Saving
& Giving

Investing for
the Future

InterVarsity Press
Downers Grove, Illinois

InterVarsity Press
P.O. Box 1400, Downers Grove, IL 60515-1426
World Wide Web: www.ivpress.com
E-mail: mail@ivpress.com

InterVarsity Press® is the book-publishing division of InterVarsity Christian Fellowship/USA®, a student movement active on campus at hundreds of universities, colleges and schools of nursing in the United States of America, and a member movement of the International Fellowship of Evangelical Students. For information about local and regional activities, write Public Relations Dept., InterVarsity Christian Fellowship/USA, 6400 Schroeder Rd., P.O. Box 7895, Madison, WI 53707-7895, or visit the IVCF website at <www.ivcf.org>.

Cover illustration: Seth Carter / SuperStock

Icons: Roberta Polfus

ISBN 0-8308-2347-6

Printed in the United States of America ∞

Library of Congress Cataloging-in-Publication Data

Wood, William C., 1952-
   Getting a grip on your money / William C. Wood.
     p. cm.
   Includes index.
   ISBN 0-8308-2347-6 (paper: alk. paper)
    1. Finance, Personal. 2. Investments. I. Title

HG179 .W5777 2002
330.024—dc21

                                                      2001059389

P	18	17	16	15	14	13	12	11	10	9	8	7	6	5	4	3	2	1
Y	15	14	13	12	11	10	09	08	07	06	05	04	03	02				

To my family and my church family

Contents

Preface

The great labor leader Samuel Gompers was once asked what unions wanted, and his answer was "More!" Many of us act as if that's all we want too: more money, more luxuries, more spending, more wealth. Yet we all know there's more to life than "more."

This book is different from other books on managing money. Many of them never question the goal of "more." Although this book shows you how to make the most of your money, it also explores our duty before God to go beyond just trying to get more.

This book is different from the others in another way too. Most books on money and finances are too complicated. They propose rules and plans so complex that most readers of these books will never follow them.

This book has two purposes: to help you simplify your life and to explore how we can all honor God with our finances. We have all seen, perhaps in ourselves, the tendency to live busy lives. These are lives complicated by our possessions and the need to have enough money to support them all, now and in the future. In a cluttered life like that, God can seem both far away and incidental to what we're doing. Simplifying our lives financially can enrich our lives spiritually. Every chapter in this book, then, is geared toward the twin goals of simplifying our lives and honoring God.

Some of this subject is about making money. I have become convinced that there are simple and powerful principles for improving people's finances, and most people will never apply them.

Why is this? It's not that these simple and powerful principles are secret. They'll seem obvious to you when you read about them. The problem is that people believe it's too complex to learn enough to improve their finances. That's understandable, given the complexity of most books on personal finance.

In truth, coming up with the perfect financial plan is incredibly difficult. But you don't need the perfect financial plan. You'll be surprised how much better a quick and simple financial plan is than no financial plan at all.

I came upon these simple and powerful principles almost by accident, as a sidelight to my job as a university professor of economics. Friends at my church and relatives began to ask me for personal financial advice. When I investigated the information available, I found that most of it is biased and misleading.

It's easy to understand why this is so. Much of the personal financial information out there is produced by people who have something to sell you—investments, insurance products and the like. On the other hand, some of the best personal financial strategies involve assets that you have to seek out. I can guarantee that if you sit back waiting to be called by a telemarketer, that call won't be offering a good financial deal.

Insiders in investment and finance understand this. Here is just one example: There is a particular type of stock investment that's most favored by those who have carefully studied the stock market. This investment has turned in superior returns for many years. You'll read about it in chapter six. Among insiders, this is obviously what new investors should put their money in. Yet choices inferior to this investment are recommended to new investors every day.

If you want to buy the funds favored by the insiders, you have to seek them out. Fortunately, I have done the seeking for you, and you only have to go to appendix one at the back of this book to get a toll-free number for buying this kind of fund.

Don't be in a hurry, though—and don't trust anyone trying to sell you an investment in a hurry. Even before investing, you can simplify and improve your finances with the techniques described in this book. In fact, I believe that many people do things backward, trying to start investing first and getting their finances in order later. Appendix two in the back of this book provides a thirteen-step checklist for improving your personal finances. The steps on this checklist are covered in order in this book.

This book contains diverse kinds of material. Some of the material is advice on personal finance and investments. Although this material is sound, and while it is backed up by economic and financial research, some parts of it amount to my advice and opinion. Other parts of the book are applications of biblical teachings. If you take the Scripture as authoritative, as I do, these applications deserve close attention. At the beginning of the scriptural applications, you'll see an icon like this one: 📖

Still other parts of the book are application of general Christian principles to our financial lives before God. They're not direct applications of Scripture, but I think you'll find that they accord with the goals we aspire to as believers. These sections are marked with the Christian life icon: ☀

I believe that everyone's life is an integrated whole. You can't really separate the spiritual from the financial, or the Christian life from the rest of life. But I think that, in this book, it's important for me to separate my opinion and advice from the scriptural applications. I claim no scriptural authority for anything but the material marked with the scriptural application icon.

The principles I'll outline are durable. They don't change with every passing financial fad. Still, it's hard to keep a book totally up-to-date. Therefore, in conjunction with this book I am operating a website, <www.plainmoney.com>. On that website I'll offer new information as it becomes available. For example, appendix one at the back of the book gives the toll-free number of the best low-cost firm in the industry for buying the kinds of investments I recommend. If that firm loses its low-cost leadership and a new firm takes that title, I'll let you know all about that new firm at my website.

Because I have written this book on a basic level, some readers will easily master the material and want to find out more. To these readers, I recommend Ron Blue's *Master Your Money* and the entire list of more advanced books on plainmoney.com. I have written on a basic level—not because I think advanced finance and economics are unimportant, but because the most basic principles are the most important for people to know.

I have in mind two sets of people who might benefit from this book. First, I would like to reach any Christian who is considering buying a secular guide on personal finance. This book should serve better because of its focus on honoring God with our finances. Second, this book will work well as a small-group resource or Sunday school lesson series for Christians who want to know the principles of sound personal finance and to integrate them with their faith.

This book originated as a series of thirteen lessons on personal finance for the Sunday school program at my home church, Beaver Creek Church of the Brethren near Bridgewater, Virginia. As I have taught and spoken on personal finance and faith, I have been struck by two things. First, I have noticed that people both inside and outside of Christian circles have a great deal of interest in simplifying their finances. I hope that my writing and teaching may attract the interest of people who have not yet heard or fully considered the gospel. Second, I have realized with new force that financial security means nothing in the absence of a right relationship with God. As Jesus Christ asked regarding unbelievers, "What will it profit them if they gain the whole world but forfeit their life? Or what will they give in return for their life?" (Matthew 16:26 NRSV).

In keeping with this book's origins as a series of Sunday school lessons, I have included study and teaching aids with each chapter, along with in-chapter reflections on the biblical implications of personal finance. The book is teachable as well as readable.

Thanks are due to several people who helped with this project. I am grateful to my mentor and former colleague, Ken Elzinga, who read the manuscript at an early stage and offered insightful comments. Frank McCraw offered detailed suggestions based on his experience in counseling and encouraging people through the Crown Ministries small-group studies in stewardship. Carlton Dixon, also a seasoned participant in Crown Ministries, helped me see how this book could fit in with existing books on stewardship and how it could usefully be different. Dr. Wayne McNett, my family doctor, stimulated my thinking in several useful conversations about the financial implications of taxes on the peace issue. Al Hsu at InterVarsity Press showed patience and good humor through the process of development and editing. I am also indebted to an anonymous reviewer for InterVarsity Press, who made suggestions that improved every chapter. Finally, my Sunday school class helped me to strengthen the manuscript throughout.

I would like to widely share the principles that can help people prosper even as they keep money in its proper place. Therefore I encourage you to pass this book along when you have finished with it. If this book can help any of us do a better job honoring God while simplifying our personal finances, that will be the greatest reward I could receive from writing this book.

1

Declare Victory & Admit Defeat

The perfect is the enemy of the good.
RUSSIAN PROVERB

ANSWER QUICKLY, AND BE HONEST: When was the last time you vacuumed your refrigerator coils? Never? Years ago? But you've probably heard, somewhere, that your refrigerator will run better if you keep the coils cleaned.

Do you check your smoke detector every week to see if it's working? You know that you should, but it's hard to remember.

Do you drink eight glasses of water a day and eat six to eleven servings of grain products? You've heard that you should.

We get overwhelmed by all the advice we get. Because we can't do everything, we do nothing. And that's a shame, because often there are a few things we can do that will really help. For example, while we *should* have all the scheduled maintenance done on our cars right on time, automotive insiders say that if we can't get everything else done, we should at least keep the oil changes and safety items up-to-date. Now, that's not the best auto maintenance plan, but it's a whole lot better than doing nothing.

Every day people make personal financial mistakes because they do nothing. Ideally, they'd work out a perfect financial plan and do what it said. But they despair of ever working out that perfect financial plan. Partly as a result, they make dumb mistakes that reduce their financial security and cause them to worry.

This book is about reducing your financial worries. A key strategy is to declare victory and admit defeat. Declare that you're going to worry less about money, but admit that you're not going to pull off the perfect financial plan. With that out of the way, you can concentrate on doing a better job of managing your money. Notice I said "a better job" of managing your money, not "the best possible job you can do."

The Russian proverb is right: the perfect *is* the enemy of the good. We probably all understand this when we're talking about something like getting in shape or losing weight. We understand that it's better to take a walk four times a week than to stay on the couch. If we said, though, "I'm staying on the couch until I'm sure that I'll do the perfect exercise plan," we'd probably stay on the couch.

In this book we'll do the financial equivalent of going for a walk four times a week. We'll be a whole lot better off than if we stayed on the couch. This means that, at times, you'll read advice in this book that's less than the theoretical best. And if you find that you want to go beyond this book's advice? Well, there are plenty of books and articles to help you with the perfect financial plan.

The Importance of a Quick Start

Why would anyone settle for a less than perfect financial plan? One good reason is that delay is costly. An imperfect plan begun early is much better than a perfect plan that gets put off.

Let's look at two people, Chris and Dusty, both twenty-five years old when the story starts.

Chris doesn't complete a full financial plan but does manage to begin putting away $100 a month through payroll deduction. Chris does this immediately and gets a 10 percent long-term return.

Dusty says, "I'm not ready for a financial plan. Maybe next year." Dusty keeps putting it off, but after five years does a great job of research and finds something that has a 12 percent long-term return. Dusty starts putting away $100 a month, just like Chris.

Chris has a head start but Dusty catches up, right? Wrong, in this example. By retirement age Chris has over $585,000 to work with. Dusty—at $581,000—has not yet quite caught up. Keep in mind, too, that as the years go by Chris might learn more about how to get high returns and might equal Dusty's 12 percent return, in which case Dusty would never catch up to Chris.

It's important to get started early. So whatever you do, promise yourself that even if you don't finish this book you'll start putting aside a small amount each month and worry about the details later.

The Power of Bounded Frittering

Once you fully understand the importance of not trying to be perfect in your financial life, you can understand the importance of what I call "bounded frittering." Bounded frittering is taking a set amount of money and spending it any way you want. You fritter it away, or spend it in a frivolous way.

Why can bounded frittering help you become a better money manager? Because it keeps you away from unbounded frittering!

Many people can stick to a budget, or manage their money better in general, if from time to time they let themselves have a little fun with a definite sum of money. Then they return to a disciplined spending plan.

It's something like going on a diet. If you start on a diet plan that starves you every day, you probably won't stick with it, and you may go back to the eating habits that caused the problem in the first place. But if you occasionally allow yourself an indulgence—say, six hundred calories to eat any way you want to—before returning to a sensible diet, you'll do better than you would on a starvation diet.

In this book you'll see how the power of bounded frittering can help you take control of your finances. Maybe not spending at all on frivolous things would be a better plan for you. But if so, you're rare. Most people respond to an extremely tight budget the same way they respond to a super-strict diet: they give up and go back to their old habits.

Getting a Little More, Not a Lot More

As an economist, I get the chance to do a lot of interesting reading. One of the most curious findings I've read concerned the happiness of lottery winners. After the initial elation fades, most lottery winners don't remain significantly happier!

Why is that? It's because we all have a little "happy-o-stat" inside, something like a thermostat. Our happy-o-stat reacts when we get some major material gain, like a new house or a better car. The happy-o-stat makes us take things for granted, so that often we're only happier for the short time right after we get something new or different.

Lottery winners feel a lot better right after they win. But then their happy-o-stat cuts in, telling them that this is their normal level of wealth and money. Pretty soon they don't feel any better than they did before they won the lottery. Some feel much worse, as they struggle with the problems that come with sudden wealth.

You can turn the happy-o-stat to your advantage. You'll be the happiest, materially, if you don't have large changes in your standard of living. So the idea is to improve your standard of living gradually over time, not to go for big gains. For example, later in this book you'll see the power of handling a debt payoff properly. If you have been paying a debt (say, a car payment) at $400 a month and one day you finish, you now have $400 a month to go out and blow. But wait! If you take that $400, give yourself some bounded frittering out of it and put the rest to work for you in an investment, you can do much better. If you blow the $400 a month, you'll feel better only for a while. Then your happy-o-stat will kick in and tell you that this extra $400 a month is normal. You'll get used to it and in time you won't be any happier than before. And on the day when your old car dies, you won't have anything saved to replace it.

You'll see there are lots of ways to go about getting a little more, not a whole lot more, when you increase your standard of living.

Why would a believer pray, "Give me neither poverty nor riches"? Because both poverty and riches have their disadvantages. One of the authors of the book of Proverbs had this to say to God:

Keep falsehood and lies far from me;
   give me neither poverty nor riches,
   but give me only my daily bread.
Otherwise, I may have too much and disown you
   and say, "Who is the LORD?"
Or I may become poor and steal,
   and so dishonor the name of my God. (Proverbs 30:8-9)

Tricking Yourself into Doing the Right Thing

Sometimes we do things that make perfect sense. We're rational. Other times we do things that don't make any sense at all. Then we're being irrational. Economic and financial behavior is a curious mix of the rational and the irrational. Therefore we are sometimes best off if we trick ourselves into doing the right thing.

Here's an example. We all know we should save. But when we come to the end of the month, there's nothing left to save. Now maybe some super-rational person can find a way to limit spending during the month and have something left to save. For most of us, though, we do better if we have the saving taken out of our paycheck before we even see it. Why does that make a difference? Couldn't we just pull that saved money out of savings and spend it anyway? Maybe we could, but most of us find it easier to have the money taken away by payroll deduction. It's harder to have all the money and then try to save some from it.

The Harvard economist Thomas Schelling did some fascinating studies about why people behave this way.* Someone who's trying to quit smoking throws away all the cigarettes in the house, even though it's likely he will fail in the plan to quit and have to restock at some expense. So why does he do it? It's a mental game, but one that has helped some people to beat the odds and quit smoking.

In managing our money, sometimes we have to fool ourselves into doing the right thing.

It's not only in seeking good financial habits that we face an internal struggle. The apostle Paul spoke for many of us when he said, "I do not understand what I do. For what I want to do I do not do, but what I hate I do" (Romans 7:15). We are all fighting a difficult battle between our best nature and our sinful nature. It pays to use every available weapon in this battle: prayer, meditation and, yes, sometimes even fooling ourselves into doing the right thing.

---

*See Thomas C. Schelling, "Self-Command in Practice, in Policy, and in a Theory of Rational Choice," *American Economic Review* 74, no. 2 (1984): 1-11; "The Intimate Contest for Self-Command," in *Choice and Consequence: Perspectives of an Errant Economist* (Cambridge, Mass.: Harvard University Press, 1984).

Putting Money in Its Place

This book is about the proper management of money. It's a subject to which I have devoted much of my professional life. However, I don't think money is the most important thing in the world. I'm not even sure it's in the top ten. Think about the times in your life when you have been the happiest and the most fulfilled. Then ask yourself how important money was to that happiness.

If you're like most of us, you're thinking about a special someone or a wonderful time together with friends—and money didn't matter much at all. If you have had a time in your life when you suddenly saw your income increase, didn't the thrill of having more to spend wear off quickly?

True happiness can't be found in better money management. Still, I think it's important. You can avoid a lot of unhappiness by staying away from bad money management.

I hope that over time you will become healthier, wealthier and wiser. In this book I'll spend more time on the "wealthier" part, but you won't be happier if you have more worries and more money. This is all about how to worry less about money and become happier in the process.

> Christians face a clear warning: If our financial affairs cause us to turn from God, we are in eternal danger. Jesus Christ warned that "the worries of this life and the deceitfulness of wealth" can choke out the message of God's kingdom just as surely as thorns choke out growing grain (Matthew 13:22). *Fool* is a strong word, but that's what God calls a person who stores up material goods and trusts in them (Luke 12:15-21).
>
> Therefore, if we ever find our financial matters getting in the way of our relationship with God, we know what to do: forget everything else and turn back to God in prayer.

One of the most important things we can do, then, is to declare victory over money by admitting defeat. We admit that we cannot and will not come up with the perfect plan, but at the same time we insist that we will worry less and loosen any hold that money may have over us.

 ## Group Study Activities and Questions

1. Along with the other participants in your study group, write down your top three financial goals—not sensitive ones, so that they're OK to share. Then pass your sheet of paper to the group leader. After the group leader has chosen one person's set of financial goals and written them on a chalkboard or flip chart, try to guess whose goals they are. (Of course, the author of the goals should not give it away at first.) Repeat with each person's goals.

a. Why did you guess that a certain person had a certain set of goals?

b. Are your goals very different from those of others in the group?

c. Do any of the goals being discussed conflict with the goal of following Christ? Could they, if pushed too far? Why or why not?

2. Make two lists. In the first one, list the top five sources of joy or satisfaction you've had in the last five years. In the second, list the top five sources of stress or worry in the last five years. Compare your lists with those of others in the group.

a. Did money show up on either list? On both lists? Why?

b. Would it be a good objective to have money show up on neither list?

3. In the chapter's example of Chris and Dusty, were you surprised that Dusty never overcame that late start to catch up with Chris? (It's surprising to most people, unless they have seen the example before.) Why don't people save more money when they're young, if it makes such a big difference to their later wealth?

4. Read Proverbs 30:7-9. Which is a more difficult spiritual problem: too much money or too little? Why? Which have you experienced more of?

5. If you played the lottery and won a $10 million payout, how much of the money would you give to the church? Why?

2

Get Control of Your Budget

*You've got to be very careful if you don't know
where you're going, because you might not get there.*
YOGI BERRA

Y OGI BERRA, THAT BASEBALL GREAT and street-corner philoso-
pher, got it right. It's important to know where you're going. And
when it comes to personal finances, that means setting goals and
thinking about a budget.

Some advisers in personal finance will tell you to track every
penny. That is, you should keep a budget and carefully record where
all your money goes. If you get cash out of your bank account to
spend, then take a little notebook and write down where it all goes.

I think that's bad advice.

Why? Because when most people try to track every penny, they
get tired of it and give up quickly. The attempt to set up the perfect
budget can get in the way of setting up a good, if imperfect, budget.
In this chapter we'll discover simple ways to take control of a budget.

Spend Less Than You Make

All the smooth financial planning in the world can't get around this one fact: if you spend all you make, you can't accomplish any financial goal (other than spending). So, to accomplish your financial goals, one vitally important thing you have to do is spend less than you make.

This seems simple, but a lot of people act as if they don't understand it. They commit to buying some big-ticket item, and the payments are so big that for months afterward they'll be spending more than they make.

Hold it! If you're in debt trouble now, you need to act right away to get control. Before this hour is done, go to the phone and call the National Foundation for Consumer Credit at 1-800-388-2227. Or look in your local yellow pages under "Credit and Debt Counseling." The counseling is always confidential and usually free. Don't wait.

If you're not in trouble but you are looking to do better with your finances, it's time to think seriously about a budget—nothing fancy, but enough to find a way to spend less than you make. There are two ways to do this: spend less or make more.

Think carefully about whether you can be making more money. You might work more overtime or seek extra pay on the job you're now working. Or you might consider changing jobs. If you are stuck in a low-paying job just because of habit, think about breaking that habit and doing something else.

Few people, however, will become better off by changing jobs. Usually, they're already in the best job they can find. More importantly, even getting a big raise can leave them no better off financially. Most people don't spend money as carefully when they have more. If they don't pay attention, they find themselves spending more on lots of little things. Surprise! At the end of the month they're as close to running out of money as ever.

The lesson? Start budgeting now, before you get that big raise or that new job. Then you can be prepared to make real progress when you start making more money.

Spend less money than you make. Since most people won't solve their financial problems by making more money, they have to do it by spending less money. That's where budgeting comes in. But make this promise to yourself before you start: *I will actually do something about my spending, even if it's small.*

Don't let yourself get trapped into making big budgeting plans, then giving up, letting bad habits take over and doing nothing. A rough budget is much better than no budget. If you start with a rough budget, you can always make it better. If you just say "I'll spend less," you probably won't change anything. That's human nature. So do some rough budgeting.

For Christians, one budget priority should be giving away at least a tenth of their income. This guideline, called a "tithe," goes back to Old Testament times but was also specifically endorsed by Jesus Christ (Matthew 23:23).

Some people feel that they can't afford to give away a tenth of their income, so they resolve to give "as much as they can" and they don't consider the amount. They don't want to think about the amount until they can afford to give a tenth. Here, the better is the enemy of the good. If you can't give a tenth, then give away a lesser amount, like 1 percent or 5 percent—and then resolve to increase your giving by 1 percent a year until you're giving away at least 10 percent.

But won't that wreck your budget? Surprisingly, no. Most people do better on 90 percent of their income if they faithfully give away a tenth. It may be that when they give away a tenth, people refocus on what's important and don't waste as much money in their monthly budget. It may be a quirk of human nature. Or it might just be one of the many ways that God works in the world. Christian financial counselors and pastors have seen it work too many times for it to be ignored.

How to Do It

When it comes to establishing a rough budget, start with this principle: No one member of a household can budget alone. Everyone has to be on board. That means all the adults and any kids who are old enough to spend money.

Before calling everybody together, it's important for someone to take the lead and do the homework. It would be great if you had detailed records of money spent, but most people don't. So here's what to do: Look at the money spent in a single month. Don't pick a month that was highly unusual for you. Just pick an ordinary month. Don't try for 100 percent accuracy because you won't achieve it anyway. Just promise yourself that you'll do a good job figuring out where the money went in that month.

Use any method that works for you. If putting sales tickets in different piles works, do that. For some people, going through the bank statement for a given month works well. You can use a table like the one you'll see in figure 2.1. It shows the spending of Matt and Jan, two young married people with children named Jared and Katie.

Let's see what we can learn by looking at Matt and Jan's checkbook register. Matt and Jan are making pretty good money—close to the national average. But they never feel that they have enough. In this month they started out fine, but they were hurt toward the end of the month when their Labor Day vacation bills came in. Close to the end of the month, Jan bought a dress, knowing that she didn't have quite enough money in checking to cover it but confident that Matt's paycheck would be deposited before that check got to the bank.

If you asked them, Matt and Jan would say they honestly don't know where all the money goes. Looking at figure 2.2, you'll see a good way of tracking where money goes. Matt and Jan just photocopied their checkbook register at the left side of a big piece of

No.	Date	Description	Payment	Deposit	Balance
	10/1	Matt's paycheck		1925.76	1925.76
1579	10/2	Wal-Mart-Katie's shirt	12.89		1912.87
1580	10/2	American Mortgage-Oct. pmt	657.05		1255.82
1581	10/3	Town of Bluff Park-water	45.10		1210.72
1582	10/4	Jiffy Lube-Matt's car	33.66		1177.06
1583	10/4	Cash	225.00		952.06
1584	10/4	Safeway-groceries	150.48		801.58
1585	10/8	Chace Lake Club-golf balls	13.93		787.65
1586	10/8	Chace Lake Club-dues	280.00		507.65
	10/10	Deposit-insurance reimb.		41.69	549.34
1587	10/13	Safeway-groceries	87.30		462.04
1588	10/16	Cash-ATM	60.00		402.04
	10/16	Jan's paycheck		1380.28	1782.32
1589	10/17	Chace Lake Club-golf umbrella	69.38		1712.94
1590	10/17	Bluff Park Exxon-Jan's car	92.93		1620.01
1592	10/17	Food Lion	36.71		1583.30
1593	10/19	Cash-ATM	100.00		1483.30
1594	10/20	Dr. Timberlake-Jared (ears)	82.32		1400.98
1595	10/21	Eckerd Drugs-Jared's Rx	35.85		1365.13
	10/21	Deposit-Matt's mileage		11.42	1376.55
1596	10/21	Wal-Mart-storage bags	17.51		1359.04
1597	10/21	Safeway-groceries	141.46		1217.58
1598	10/21	Master Card-Chace Lake Club	67.41		1150.17
1599	10/21	South Central Bell-ph. bill	48.90		1101.27
1600	10/21	Cash-ATM	85.00		1016.27
1601	10/24	Am. Express-hotel at beach	246.90		769.37
1602	10/24	VISA-trip to beach	454.05		315.32
1603	10/27	Food Lion-groceries	70.71		244.61
1604	10/28	Cash-ATM	100.00		144.61
1606	10/28	Atlantic Power-elec. bill	95.97		48.64
1607	10/28	Belk-Jan's dress	144.15		-95.51
Totals and ending balance			3454.66	3359.15	-95.51

Figure 2.1. Matt and Jan's checkbook register

paper, then drew some lines to make additional columns. Then they took each checkbook entry and wrote down the number of dollars again in one of the columns. For example, that first check to Wal-Mart for Katie's shirt went into the "Clothing" column for $12.89; the next one to American Mortgage went into the "Housing" column; and so on.

They totaled the columns. Then they divided total "Food" expenditures by total income to find that they were spending 14 percent of their income on food. They did the same math on the other columns. When they were done, they had a much better idea of where the money was going.

Figure 2.3 shows another revealing view of Matt and Jan's finances. They classified all their spending again. But this time, instead of considering food, clothing, shelter and the like, they looked at how much they had spent on what they said was important to them. (They had made the list at a marriage encounter retreat.) They discovered a mismatch between their values and their spending. They had said that giving and personal growth were very important values to them, but they found in October they had spent nothing on either.

You may be thinking that Matt and Jan's financial life is very different from yours. That's probably right. But some common patterns occur when people take a close look at their spending for a month:

☐ They often find that they're spending a lot on "cash." They're getting cash from the ATM or writing checks to cash, after which it's hard to say where the money went.

☐ They often find that reducing expenditures on food from the grocery store isn't the key to solving their financial problems. When people are trying to cut back on their spending, their first impulse is often to say, "We'll spend less at the grocery store." For people who aren't shopping carefully, that's a good thought—and Matt and Jan could do better here. Still, most people can't save as much at the

No.	Date	Description	Payment	Deposit	Balance
	10/1	Matt's paycheck		1925.76	1925.76
1579	10/2	Wal-Mart-Katie's shirt	12.89		1912.87
1580	10/2	American Mortgage-Oct. pmt	657.05		1255.82
1581	10/3	Town of Bluff Park-water	45.10		1210.72
1582	10/4	Jiffy Lube-Matt's car	33.66		1177.06
1583	10/4	Cash	225.00		952.06
1584	10/4	Safeway-groceries	150.49		801.58
1585	10/8	Chace Lake Club-golf balls	13.93		787.65
1586	10/8	Chace Lake Club-dues	280.00		507.65
	10/10	Deposit-insurance reimb.		41.69	549.34
1587	10/13	Safeway-groceries	87.30		462.04
1588	10/16	Cash-ATM	60.00		402.04
	10/16	Jan's paycheck		1380.28	1782.32
1589	10/17	Chace Lake Club-golf umbrella	69.38		1712.94
1590	10/17	Bluff Park Exxon-Jan's car	92.93		1620.01
1592	10/17	Food Lion	36.71		1583. 30
1593	10/19	Cash-ATM	100.00		1483.30
1594	10/20	Dr. Timberlake-Jared (ears)	82.32		1400.98
1595	10/21	Eckerd Drugs-Jared's Rx	35.85		1365.13
	10/21	Deposit-Matt's mileage		11.42	1376.55
1596	10/21	Wal-Mart-storage bags	17.51		1359.04
1597	10/21	Safeway-groceries	141.46		1217.58
1598	10/21	Master Card-Chace Lake Club	67.41		1150.17
1599	10/21	South Central Bell-ph. bill	48.90		1101.27
1600	10/21	Cash-ATM	85.00		1016.27
1601	10/24	Am. Express-hotel at beach	246.90		769.37
1602	10/24	VISA-trip to beach	454.05		315.32
1603	10/27	Food Lion-groceries	70.71		244.61
1604	10/28	Cash-ATM	100.00		144.61
1606	10/28	Atlantic Power-elec. bill	95.97		48.64
1607	10/28	Belk-Jan's dress	144.15		-95.51
Totals and ending balance			3454.66	3359.15	-95.51
Percentages					

Figure 2.2. Budget exercise

Food	Clothing	Shelter	Utils	Transp	MedCare	Rec/Ent	Cash	Misc
	12.89							
		657.05						
			45.10					
				33.66				
							225.00	
150.48								
						13.93		
						280.00		
87.30								
							60.00	
						69.38		
				92.93				
36.71								
							100.00	
					82.32			
					35.85			
								17.51
141.46								
						67.41		
			48.90					
							85.00	
						246.90		
						454.05		
70.71								
							100.00	
			95.97					
	144.15							
486.66	157.04	657.05	189.97	126.59	118.17	1131.67	570.00	17.51
14%	5%	20%	6%	4%	4%	34%	17%	1%

6. If you're going on a diet, is it smart to throw out all of the high-calorie treats that are currently in the house? Why or why not?

7. Read Matthew 16:24-27. Would we approach our jobs and careers any differently if we promised ourselves to faithfully follow this teaching?

No.	Date	Description	Payment	Deposit	Balance
	10/1	Matt's paycheck		1925.76	1925.76
1579	10/2	Wal-Mart-Katie's shirt	12.89		1912.87
1580	10/2	American Mortgage-Oct. pmt	657.05		1255.82
1581	10/3	Town of Bluff Park-water	45.10		1210.72
1582	10/4	Jiffy Lube-Matt's car	33.66		1177.06
1583	10/4	Cash	225.00		952.06
1584	10/4	Safeway-groceries	150.48		801.58
1585	10/8	Chace Lake Club-golf balls	13.93		787.65
1586	10/8	Chace Lake Club-dues	280.00		507.65
	10/10	Deposit-insurance reimb.		41.69	549.34
1587	10/13	Safeway-groceries	87.30		462.04
1588	10/16	Cash-ATM	60.00		402.04
	10/16	Jan's paycheck		1380.28	1782.32
1589	10/17	Chace Lake Club-golf umbrella	69.38		1712.94
1590	10/17	Bluff Park Exxon-Jan's car	92.93		1620.01
1592	10/17	Food Lion	36.71		1583. 30
1593	10/19	Cash-ATM	100.00		1483.30
1594	10/20	Dr. Timberlake-Jared (ears)	82.32		1400.98
1595	10/21	Eckerd Drugs-Jared's Rx	35.85		1365.13
	10/21	Deposit-Matt's mileage		11.42	1376.55
1596	10/21	Wal-Mart-storage bags	17.51		1359.04
1597	10/21	Safeway-groceries	141.46		1217.58
1598	10/21	Master Card-Chace Lake Club	67.41		1150.17
1599	10/21	South Central Bell-ph. bill	48.90		1101.27
1600	10/21	Cash-ATM	85.00		1016.27
1601	10/24	Am. Express-hotel at beach	246.90		769.37
1602	10/24	VISA-trip to beach	454.05		315.32
1603	10/27	Food Lion-groceries	70.71		244.61
1604	10/28	Cash-ATM	100.00		144.61
1606	10/28	Atlantic Power-elec. bill	95.97		48.64
1607	10/28	Belk-Jan's dress	144.15		-95.51
Totals and ending balance			3454.66	3359.15	-95.51
Percentages					

Figure 2.3. Values exercise

Marriage	Children	Giving	P. Growth	All else
	12.89			
				657.05
				45.10
				33.66
				225.00
				150.48
13.93				
280.00				
				87.30
				60.00
69.38				
				92.93
				36.71
				100.00
	82.32			
	35.85			
				17.51
				141.46
67.41				
				48.90
				85.00
	246.90			
	454.05			
				70.71
				100.00
				95.97
				144.15
430.72	832.01			2191.93
13%	25%	0%	0%	65%

grocery store as they can elsewhere. Some families will work hard to save $5 in the grocery store but then spend $10 for fast food because they ran out of time and had to get something. This is not to say "Don't buy fast food" or "Don't allow yourself some nice food items at the store"; rather, it's to say that most people who plan to cut back at the grocery store—and there alone—won't save much money.

☐ They are surprised to find that they spend a whole lot more on some things than they thought. For Matt and Jan, it was golf. That's obvious when you look at the checkbook, but—believe it or not!—it wasn't obvious to Matt and Jan before they sat down and did this exercise. They were spending money on country club dues, golf equipment and the like. In addition, they also had to incur a minimum tab each month for food at the club or be billed for the difference. For Matt and Jan, golf was where the money was going; it will probably be something different for you.

☐ They are surprised to find that some of the things they like best don't really cost much. When Matt and Jan thought about it, they remembered how much they like taking Katie and Jared to the park with fast food. (Jan had an idealized picture of a park picnic, in which she packed the perfect picnic into a basket with a red-checked tablecloth. But preparing that picnic would take hours, so she never did it. The perfect was the enemy of the good.)

What Next?

When you know where your money's going, what then? Remember that your goal is to spend less money than you make. Now that you know where the money's going, you have done the hard part. Call the household together and show everyone where the money went.

Usually, when you all look at the summary, some things will jump off the page at you and you'll see how to spend less—and without sacrificing a whole lot of happiness. Matt and Jan actually felt liberated when they gave up their membership at the golf club. They were rediscovering something G. K. Chesterton said long ago: "There are two ways to get enough. One is to continue to accumulate more and more. The other is to desire less."

From around the table, you may hear everyone say that they can't cut back on their spending at all. They may think they "need" everything they're now buying. If so, have everyone consider this: there's a family down the street from you right now, in similar circumstances, that's getting by on 10 percent less than you are. If you changed your spending to match, you could put away 10 percent of your income. Your household is probably making 10 percent more than it did at some time in the past. You made it then, didn't you? If you could just freeze your spending at what it was before, you could be putting away 10 percent of your household income. All of you need to be honest with each other about what you need.

At this point, you have a decision to make. You will improve your finances more quickly and more dramatically if you write down your goals and track your progress. (For more information on how, buy and use Ron Blue's *Master Your Money* or any of the budgeting books listed at plainmoney.com.) But if that thought makes you consider doing nothing and lapsing back into your former spending habits, think for a minute. Don't give up! Decide that you'll do one positive thing for your budget from what you have learned, and go from there. You can improve your finances without detailed budgeting.

Trick Yourself into Saving Money

Maybe there are some smart, perfect budgeters somewhere. I'm not one of them, and you're probably not either. Most of us have to trick ourselves into saving money. The best tricks rely on this principle: When we have money, we spend it; if we don't think we have it, we don't spend it. You can turn this part of human nature to your advantage by hiding money from yourself. If you have an automatic savings plan at work, use it. If you have the ability to automatically divert some of your money into a savings account on payday, use that.

Here's another way to trick yourself into saving money. Let's say you have a debt that you're paying off, such as a car payment. When that debt ends, keep paying—only pay yourself instead of the lender. Keep making out that monthly check, but make it payable to yourself and put it into your savings account. Better yet, get the money automatically deducted and put into savings before you ever see it.

Some time or another you'll have to replace that car. When you do, it will be so much better to have money saved. If you decide to live high on that car payment money after the debt is gone, you'll have to cut back when it's time to buy something new.

When we have trouble controlling our spending, the most important step is prayer. God honors our prayers, even if we're not sure what we should be praying for (Romans 8:26). This is especially important for couples making joint decisions on finances—or on anything else, for that matter. Tricking ourselves into saving more is just a strategy that will help us succeed. There is no trick, no strategy, nothing we can do that's as powerful as what God can do in us and through us.

Let's be clear about one thing: The point of tricking yourself into saving money is not to spend your time worrying about how to accumulate more money. Rather, the point is to avoid worrying about how to accumulate money. Make it automatic, occurring out of sight, and you'll be less likely to worry about it.

Remember that you're following a biblical instruction if you provide for your family. "If anyone does not provide for his relatives, and especially for his immediate family, he has denied the faith and is worse than an unbeliever" (1 Timothy 5:8). But if saving causes you to focus on getting and having more, you're making a mistake. The whole point of a saving plan is to remove our focus from money, in that way conforming our lives to what Jesus said: "Do not worry about tomorrow, for tomorrow will worry about itself. Each day has enough trouble of its own" (Matthew 6:34).

Some authors recommend taking all the coins you get in change every week and depositing them (instead of keeping them in a sock drawer). The principle is the same: to trick yourself into saving money without putting yourself on the financial equivalent of a starvation diet.

The Importance of Controlling Fixed Costs

One of the most common mistakes I have seen people make in household budgeting is letting their fixed costs get too high. "Fixed costs" are, well, fixed. Each month they're the same amount no matter what you do. For many people, rent or mortgage payments are the largest fixed costs. For other people, the largest fixed cost every month is a car payment.

Fixed costs take away your maneuvering room in a budget. Each month you have to pay them. You can't tell the bank, "I didn't use my car much at all this month, so I'm skipping the payment."

Here's a common mistake that people make: They look for housing to rent or buy and they decide to stretch beyond what they're comfortable paying. At first all goes well and they enjoy their new apartment or home. But over time they begin to regard their nicer quarters as the norm. They take it for granted. Meanwhile, that payment is due every month. Because they have stretched beyond what they're comfortable paying, anything unexpected causes them to come up short of money. Worse yet, they begin worrying about money.

The same thing often happens with cars. The monthly payment continues, no matter what. But after a time, people come to regard that car as "usual" or "normal" or what they're entitled to.

It may seem that this advice just says, "Don't spend money." But if you put yourself on a starvation budget, you probably won't stick to it anyway, and you wouldn't be happy about it. So the advice is this: try to channel your indulgences toward things that aren't fixed costs.

Is there an occasion for celebration? Then celebrate! Celebrate with a grand party or a night out or whatever. Set aside some money in advance, and then spend that amount frivolously. Just don't celebrate by signing up for something that will push your fixed costs every month beyond your comfort zone.

Allowing for Surprises: Your SIT Fund

Life is full of surprises. How can anyone have a budget when life is that way? The answer is to have an SIT fund. SIT stands for two things: (1) *sit* down when you get an unexpected bill, and (2) surprises, insurance and taxes.

First, people too often panic when they get a bill and don't have the money to cover it. They end up making a mistake, like borrowing money on unfavorable terms. That's why it's important to sit down—that is, stop and think carefully—when you get an unexpected bill.

Second, since you know you're going to have surprises, insurance and taxes, it's better to prepare for them in advance. Make a rough guess about how much you have paid in surprises, insurance and taxes in the last year. Then divide that by the number of paychecks you'll have and put that much money into savings each time you get paid.

I'll say more about the SIT fund in chapters to come, but for now think about one of the best uses of an SIT fund: to avoid giving money away to the government. That's what you're actually doing if you have lots of money withheld from your paycheck to get a big tax refund. That's just like giving the government the use of your money all year, until you finally file your income tax. It's better to fill out the tax forms to figure your withholding correctly. If that reduces your amount withheld by, say, $50 per paycheck, *don't* just let that $50 get into your checking account or your pocket. Instead, trick yourself into saving it by having it automatically routed into a savings account.

Someone I know does this. Every year at tax time he files the forms, gets a small refund or pays a small amount of tax—and then gives himself a big "virtual tax refund" from the SIT fund! Before, he used to let the government have the money all year, then congratulate himself on getting a big refund in the spring. Now he gets a virtual tax refund in the spring, and higher interest on his savings all year, because he's not having taxes overwithheld.

 The apostle James warned about assuming too much about our financial futures.

Now listen, you who say, "Today or tomorrow we will go to this or that city, spend a year there, carry on business and make money." Why, you do not even know what will happen tomorrow. What is your life? You are a mist that appears for a little while and then vanishes. (James 4:13-14)

Helps put things into perspective, doesn't it? The point of saving and budgeting is not to plan out our financial futures but to avoid worrying about them. Having a fund for surprises, insurance and taxes helps us to avoid worry.

As James concluded, "Instead, you ought to say, 'If it is the Lord's will, we will live and do this or that' " (James 4:15).

Debt: Is It a Problem?

You may have been motivated to look at your budget because you're uncomfortable with your debt. Should you be? In some cases the answer will be obvious, because you're dodging bill collectors. In other cases, though, people will be getting into in trouble with debt but won't know it. Here's a good rule to keep debt from sneaking up on you: Don't finance anything for longer than its useful life.

What happens when people don't follow this rule? They do things like putting a car on a home equity loan that lasts for fifteen years. The car may be junk after ten years, but they're still paying for it for five more. Or they charge a vacation and take a year to finally pay off the credit card bills. Even after the vacation is just a memory, they have eleven more months of bills to pay. In fact, most of what people have long-term on credit cards has already been consumed. They're violating the rule that says not to finance anything for longer than its useful life.

When all that's left of a spending spree is the debt, the minimum payment on that debt has become a fixed cost. You have to pay it regularly. It reduces your flexibility and lays a burden on you. You will have qualified for the credit at each stage, but then you find yourself with bills you can't pay. What then?

Debt Reduction

When you can't pay your debts, or if you have financed things for longer than their useful life, you need to take action. Some would say you need a "debt reduction plan." You do, but if phrasing it that way makes it sound like a lot of work, hold on.

You won't have to do hours of planning to make a positive difference on your debt. Instead, do this:

1. Resolve that you won't get in any deeper. This is not only the first but also the most important step. To make progress, you have to stop acquiring new debts.

2. Write down all your debts, the amount owed, the interest rate and the minimum monthly payment.

3. Add up all the minimum monthly payments. That amount is the least you'll need to service your debt. Don't think about skipping payments; that would only make things worse.

4. Now start paying off the debts. Cut unnecessary expenses out of your budget using the approach outlined in this chapter. Start by paying off a small debt, such as a $200 credit card balance. Then don't charge any more on that card. Continue until you have paid off any debt that's for a longer term than the useful

life of what you bought using it.

That's it! It will take time, but you can do it.

Just as getting into debt or using credit cards is addictive, try to make knocking off debt addictive for you. Didn't it feel good to take that little debt on the credit card down to zero? Now set your sights on the highest-interest-rate debt you have. Start making more than the minimum payment, and keep on until it's gone.

Mathematically, you save the most money if you pay off the highest-interest-rate debt first. Psychologically, though, it's good to knock off a small debt first, just to experience the feeling of taking a balance to zero and keeping it there.

If you're in debt trouble, it probably took years for you to get there. Don't try to go too fast in getting out. Remember, the perfect is the enemy of the good. If you try the "perfect" debt reduction plan, it may not work any better than a starvation diet in weight loss. Sure, you get quick results, but you can't keep it up.

The Case of Student Loans

Student loans, for most people considering them, are a good deal. They help you to finance an "asset" with a long and productive life—higher education, along with the greater salary that it brings. Even a long-term payback period doesn't violate the rule that says don't finance anything for longer than its useful life.

In a debt reduction plan, you should treat student loans just like any other debt. If you have a small student loan, consider the psychological lift of taking it to zero. If you have larger student loans, list them along with all your other debts. Generally student loans will have a lower interest rate than your other debts, so you'll be knocking off the other debts first. But as you slowly pay down a student loan, don't get impatient. Remember that it financed an asset that's valuable for life. Far more people get in trouble with credit cards than with excessive student loans.

Debt reduction is commended in the first part of Romans 13:8: "Let no debt remain outstanding, except the continuing debt to love one another." Notice that the passage assumes the existence of debt but calls for it to be extinguished. Notice also that this teaching is more about love than it is about finance.

Debt reduction is a good idea, but loving others is vital as we follow the example of Christ: "Be imitators of God . . . as dearly loved children and live a life of love, just as Christ loved us and gave himself up for us as a fragrant offering and sacrifice to God" (Ephesians 5:1-2).

The Importance of Doing Something

Many people read budgeting advice like what's in this chapter and decide they'll wait to budget. Don't wait! Promise yourself that you'll take one small step toward getting better control of your budget right now. Think about the tiniest step that you will in fact accomplish. That tiny step is better than the perfect budget, if you never would get started on that perfect budget.

 Group Study Activities and Questions

1. Figure 2.4 at the end of this chapter is a copy of Matt and Jan's checkbook register and, to the right, some empty boxes. Using the empty spaces, divide up the budget into (1) marriage, (2) children, (3) giving, (4) personal growth and (5) everything else. (This has already been done for you in figure 2.3, but don't look there. It's good for you to go through the exercise of apportioning expenses among different value categories.)

a. Matt and Jan say that marriage, children and giving are their top personal values. Does their budget agree?

b. If you don't spend much on something, does that mean you don't value it? Why or why not?

c. If you did this exercise with your own checkbook, what would it say about your spending and your values?

2. Which is easier for you as you think about spending less than you make: (1) spending less or (2) making more? Do you think it's the same way for most people? Why or why not?

3. Read Matthew 23:23. What does this verse say to Christians today as they think about whether to give away a tenth, more than a tenth or less than a tenth of their income?

4. Many people feel that they spend as much money as they get, no matter what that amount is. As a result, while they may receive pay raises that add up to a lot over the years, they don't end up saving any more money. Why is that? Why do most people save money more easily if they never see it (for example, if it's taken out of their paycheck before they're paid)?

5. Does most of your debt finance long-term assets, like a car or a house? Or is it just the product of spending on things like vacations that are here today and gone tomorrow? What's the problem with financing things for longer than their useful life?

6. Read 1 Timothy 5:8, then 5:3-10 (the surrounding verses) for context. Do these verses obligate you to support your brother if he is in need? What if he is in need because he's lazy and never wants to work?

No.	Date	Description	Payment	Deposit	Balance
	10/1	Matt's paycheck		1925.76	1925.76
1579	10/2	Wal-Mart-Katie's shirt	12.89		1912.87
1580	10/2	American Mortgage-Oct. pmt	657.05		1255.82
1581	10/3	Town of Bluff Park-water	45.10		1210.72
1582	10/4	Jiffy Lube-Matt's car	33.66		1177.06
1583	10/4	Cash	225.00		952.06
1584	10/4	Safeway-groceries	150.48		801.58
1585	10/8	Chace Lake Club-golf balls	13.93		787.65
1586	10/8	Chace Lake Club-dues	280.00		507.65
	10/10	Deposit-insurance reimb.		41.69	549.34
1587	10/13	Safeway-groceries	87.30		462.04
1588	10/16	Cash-ATM	60.00		402.04
	10/16	Jan's paycheck		1380.28	1782.32
1589	10/17	Chace Lake Club-golf umbrella	69.38		1712.94
1590	10/17	Bluff Park Exxon-Jan's car	92.93		1620.01
1592	10/17	Food Lion	36.71		1583. 30
1593	10/19	Cash-ATM	100.00		1483.30
1594	10/20	Dr. Timberlake-Jared (ears)	82.32		1400.98
1595	10/21	Eckerd Drugs-Jared's Rx	35.85		1365.13
	10/21	Deposit-Matt's mileage		11.42	1376.55
1596	10/21	Wal-Mart-storage bags	17.51		1359.04
1597	10/21	Safeway-groceries	141.46		1217.58
1598	10/21	Master Card-Chace Lake Club	67.41		1150.17
1599	10/21	South Central Bell-ph. bill	48.90		1101.27
1600	10/21	Cash-ATM	85.00		1016.27
1601	10/24	Am. Express-hotel at beach	246.90		769.37
1602	10/24	VISA-trip to beach	454.05		315.32
1603	10/27	Food Lion-groceries	70.71		244.61
1604	10/28	Cash-ATM	100.00		144.61
1606	10/28	Atlantic Power-elec. bill	95.97		48.64
1607	10/28	Belk-Jan's dress	144.15		-95.51
Totals and ending balance			3454.66	3359.15	-95.51
Percentages					

Figure 2.4. Budget exercise

3

Insurance & Banking

We'll just have to live through it. Then we'll know.
W. H. DUDLEY, on the uncertainty of weather forecasts

OFTEN, WHEN PEOPLE START ON A BUDGET or a financial plan, they want to know, "When's the part where I get rich in the stock market?" Actually, that's close to the end of the process. When it comes to getting rich through investments, many people start wrong and never recover. While we're leading up to the material on the stock market, though, make sure that you never buy an investment over the phone from someone who found you. The best investment strategies are simple, but you have to initiate the contact with the investment company (using a toll-free phone number). Those who find you and call you generally have inferior investment services to offer. That's why they're calling. Anyone who shopped around would never choose unfavorable terms like those they're offering.

In fact, the reason that we're dealing with insurance and banking now is that you should have these things in order before you successfully invest money. Many people have lost big money because (1) they got into the stock market too soon or (2) they bought stock over the phone from someone who found them. At the same time, it's important to start your plan early, so that the power of investments to grow over time works in your favor. So resolve that you'll keep reading and get your banking and insurance in order.

Remember, too, that a major goal of doing all this is to worry less. Getting your insurance and banking in order can help you do just that.

The Modern Barn Raising

People in rural communities used to take care of each other. If someone's barn burned down, the entire community would turn out for a barn raising. Everyone would work at an assigned job: some doing the site preparation, some doing the heavy construction, others cooking and watching the children. Before long, a new barn would stand where the old one had burned down.

The most important feature of the barn raising was that everyone would chip in something, so that no one would have to suffer a large and uncompensated loss. Although the details are different, that's the way insurance works today. Instead of contributing labor or materials for a burned barn, we pay an insurance premium. Instead of having all the neighbors over if we suffer a loss, we file a claim with the insurance company. In the end, the result is the same: no one has to suffer a large and uncompensated loss.

This is sometimes hard to see, mainly because of the role of the insurance company. The company collects the premiums and pays the claims. Some will mourn the loss of community involved with that, in that we no longer work directly to help a neighbor in a time of loss—and I agree with that sentiment. Some will resent the profit that the insurance company gets in return for its service of pooling our premium money and paying the claims—and I understand that sentiment too. However, in a large and complex society like ours it's hard to imagine neighborhood house raising parties successfully taking the place of fire insurance on houses. So we rely on the current method of pooling risk, or insurance.

Some people believe that buying insurance indicates a lack of trust in God. I'm sure that's possible. Surely also we must trust our ultimate well-being to God. I don't have the answer to this, but I will pose some questions and answers: Is it wrong for someone whose barn burns to accept the help of neighbors? (Probably not. Those neighbors might well be following Christ in lending their assistance.) Is it wrong for a group of barn owners to pledge together that they will help each other rebuild if one of their barns burns? (Probably not; again they're just pledging assistance.) Would it be wrong for those barn owners to hire a good structural carpenter if a barn rebuilding called for that specialty? (Probably not, if they dealt fairly with that carpenter.) Would it be wrong for the barn owners to have repair materials on hand that could be used for their own barns or a neighbor's barn? (Probably not.) Would it be wrong for the barn owners to have their hired workers sometimes manage the repair materials? (Again, probably not.)

But if we have barn owners who band together and take steps to be ready to rebuild neighbors' barns, these people have in effect formed the Barn Owners' Mutual Insurance Company. The only substantial difference between their little enterprise and a modern insurance company is the nature of the organization. What's more, the modern company, by specializing in what it does, offers the pooling of risk at a lower cost to the barn owners than they could have achieved on their own. Economically, buying insurance is very much like taking part in an old-fashioned barn raising.

What lesson do we draw from those who believe it is wrong to buy insurance? I respect their beliefs, and the one thing we certainly can agree on is this: whether we buy insurance or not, our hope and trust must be in God, not in insurance. The worst hazards are hazards of the spirit, not possibilities that we will lose some possession to an accident.

Insure Against Insurable Risks

Having gotten control of your budget, the next task for you is to insure against your insurable risks. There are many underinsured people, and you don't want to be one of them. We'll see that when you start saving and investing money, it's best to leave that money alone. With the right insurance, you won't run much risk of needing that money to pay the damage from an insurable event. The rule, then, is to insure against your major insurable risks.

Sometimes insuring against your major insurable risks is automatic. For example, some major insurable risks come from car accidents: the risks that you would be hurt, that someone else would be hurt or that the accident would cause a lot of damage. In most states you have to have proof of insurance, or participate in some state alternative for insurance, in order to drive.

Everyone faces the risk of an illness or injury that would cost a lot of money for treatment and lost time at work. If you have health insurance through your work, count yourself fortunate. If you don't, then plan on getting health insurance somehow. The rates for individual health insurance aren't nearly as good as employers' group rates, but going without health insurance is inviting financial disaster.

For young income earners, a major risk is premature death that would leave dependents without enough income. Against that risk, you can buy what's known as "term life insurance." It covers you for a specified term. When that term is over, ordinarily you can continue the coverage at rates based on your age. Or—when there's no longer anyone depending on your income—you can let it lapse. (For a starting point on how much to buy, multiply your income by 6 and consider that policy amount. Someone making $40,000 per year should look at a policy amount of around $240,000.)

Young income earners who can't afford enough insurance should at least have some. There are policies that have a small face value but allow increased coverage without having to take a physical. These policies allow you to insure your insurability. This is a case where some insurance of the right kind is a whole lot better than no insurance at all.

For a young family with one of the adults (usually the mother) staying home with the kids, a major risk is this parent's premature death. Here the financial risk is not a loss of income but rather the loss of what a stay-at-home mother or father does. Term life insurance can cover the financial risk by providing the money that would be needed to hire child care, cleaning and other services. The hired services would be a poor substitute for the missing parent, to be sure, but they would have to be paid for somehow.

Think about what your major insurable risks are, and then see what the insurance industry has to cover these risks. Don't get ahead of yourself. You're not investing yet, and many of the "investment products" offered through the insurance industry aren't as good as the investments we'll discuss in a later chapter. For most people, term insurance is the best deal because it provides the most protection for your money. Whole life insurance, unlike term insurance, lasts until your death. It's much more expensive because it's part insurance, part investment.

Most whole life insurance policies aren't an especially good deal. So concentrate on using insurance to cover risks, not to save or invest money. Your goal is to get the most protection for your money, and keep looking until you find an insurance agent or company that will respect that goal and help you work toward it.

You Don't Want to Collect

Once you understand that insurance is about controlling risks, you can see why you don't want to collect. Ideally, you want to just keep paying and paying the insurance company and never get anything back. Here's why:

1. For you to collect, something bad has to happen. Risk is the probability that something bad will happen. Even though you have auto insurance, you should drive just as carefully as if you were facing financial ruin in the event of a car accident. Even though you have homeowner's insurance, you should be as careful not to burn your house down as you would if that event would make you homeless.

2. The insurance doesn't cover it all. If you suffer a $500 loss and receive a $500 payment, are you equally well off? Usually not, because of the hassle of dealing with the loss. It's better not to have the loss happen at all, if it's preventable.

3. If you collect on everyday risks, your deductible is too low. In insurance, the deductible is the amount you pay before your insurance kicks in. If you had a $1,000 accident in your car and your deductible happened to be $100, then you'd pay the first $100 and insurance would cover the other $900. If you find that you have set up your insurance to cover almost all your losses—with low deductibles—you're cheating yourself. You're paying the insurance company to cover your little risks, and that's expensive. Insurance for big risks is a better deal.

Remember the example of the barn raising? Neighbors would pitch in to help each other when one neighbor's barn burned. They wouldn't pitch in when one neighbor's milk bucket turned over or when one row of corn got blown over in a storm. Those small losses could more economically be absorbed by the household that had the small misfortune.

If you have some zero-deductible insurance, thinking that you "want to get some money back" rather than just pay insurance, that's an expensive choice. It costs the insurance company a lot to process small claims, and that cost gets built into the rate you pay for insurance that covers small losses.

This is the place where your SIT fund, covering surprises, insurance and taxes, can be a big help. Try this: Get a quote on insurance with higher deductibles all around. You'll lower your insurance payments considerably. Take the savings—this is important!—and put them in your SIT fund. Unless your luck is unusually bad, your SIT fund will build up so fast that you can easily handle small losses from that fund, without the hassle of dealing with an insurance claims procedure.

I know someone who did this with his car insurance. Some time after he raised all his deductibles, the windshield broke from a winter storm, forcing him to have it replaced. He said it hurt a lot to have to pay $300 out of his pocket—but it was actually from his SIT fund, which was already more than $300 higher because of his earlier insurance savings.

The lesson is this: Don't think of insurance as something you want to "pay you back." You're the best off if you pay and pay, never collecting.

Mattresses, Checking Accounts and Other Bad Places to Keep Money

This book is about simplifying your finances to take the worry out. Your bank is an important part of this, but in general you'll find that doing less with your bank is better than doing more.

The one thing at which banks excel is keeping money safe. Banking regulations and laws have been set up so that it's almost impossible to lose money that's been deposited in a bank. Therefore, if your only fear is losing your money, the best place for your money is a bank. No individual customer has ever lost even one penny of federally insured bank deposits since federal deposit insurance was set up. You don't need to worry about the money you have in a bank checking account, and you can use it to conduct your ordinary financial business.

Most people face a number of risks, though—and not just the risk of a bank losing their money. If you think only about the risk of losing your money and not about some other risks, you'll make mistakes. The most common of these mistakes is keeping too much money in checking. How is it possible to have too much money in the bank? That's easy—if you keep more money than you need in checking, you're losing interest that you could be earning.

I know about a retired couple who sold a piece of land, hoping to live off the proceeds for years. They kept the entire amount in a non-interest-bearing checking account. The money ran out after a number of years, but it didn't need to; the money could have replenished itself if it had been productively invested. Especially among older people, there's a fear of having money anywhere but in the bank. It's easy to see why that fear is there, but if you give in to that fear, you're taking a big risk of another sort. You're taking the risk of running out of money.

Keeping large amounts of money in a regular checking account is like burying the money in the ground. It doesn't earn any interest.

The folly of keeping money in a non-interest-bearing form has been well understood since biblical times. Remember the parable of the talents (Matthew 25:14-30)? A man entrusted some money to three servants, two of whom went out and industriously put the money to work. The third man buried the money in the ground, where it gained no interest. When all three of the men had to give account of how they had handled the money, the first two were rewarded. The man who had buried the money was punished—as the parable pointed out, he could at least have deposited the money for interest (Matthew 25:27).

Jesus was using the parable to make a spiritual point, but it also shows a long-understood financial point: it is foolish to keep wealth in a form that prevents it from growing.

Even worse than burying money in the ground is keeping it at home ("in your mattress"). In this case, the money isn't earning interest, and it's also jeopardizing your personal safety if the wrong person finds out where you're keeping the money.

All this means that everyone should have a regular checking account. Beyond your regular checking account, however, banks want to offer you a whole lot more these days. Most of what the banks offer you is not the best deal. Let's look at several examples.

"Free" checking. Free checking can turn out to be expensive for bank customers if it requires you to hold a large minimum balance in your account. I know someone who kept $10,000 in a bank account to get "free" checking. If she had kept a smaller amount in checking and put the rest of the money to work, she could have received hundreds of dollars in additional interest.

Savings. Banks offer savings accounts, and they're as safe as can be. However, the interest they pay is frequently less than half what you can get by putting your money elsewhere.

Money market funds. Money market funds are a great idea. The idea is that a financial institution pools the money of many investors, then puts that money into safe places, like U.S. government securities and top-grade corporate bonds. It passes along the interest from holding those securities and manages the flow of money into and out of the fund. Typically, you can withdraw money from a fund like this just by writing a check.

Money market funds offer greater interest and excellent access to your funds. I recommend that you keep your SIT fund (remember: surprises, insurance, taxes) in a money market account.

It's possible that in a financial catastrophe money market funds would lose value. It's always possible, for example, that the U.S. government and financial institutions would fail. In a catastrophe like that, however, your money market fund would probably be the least of your worries.

Banks sometimes offer "money market checking" or other pale imitations of a true money market fund. A quick check of interest rates will show you why the bank is not usually your best choice for a money market fund.

Check with the company listed in appendix one in the back of this book to set up an account in a money market fund.

> My church had an organ fund for several years to collect donations for replacing our aging sanctuary organ. At first, it was being kept in a bank savings account. I convinced the church to move it to a true money market account, where the money earned hundreds of dollars more interest than it would have at the bank. Our goal of replacing the organ was substantially advanced by moving the money to where it earned higher interest. This was done with minimal risk, as the money was held with a reliable major money market fund that was investing in U.S. government-backed securities.

The theme of this book is simplicity, so I'm not going to offer the common advice of shopping around for hours on end, comparing terms until you find the very best banking deal available to you. You probably don't feel that you have time to do that anyway. Instead I'll just advise you to avoid the big mistakes. Don't keep thousands of idle dollars in a checking account, and don't get taken in by "free" banking packages.

You may think that anyone with thousands of idle dollars in checking is probably financially well off, so that he or she doesn't need advice. I would have thought so, too, before I came into contact with a number of relatively poor individuals who had sold an asset or received an inheritance. As poor individuals, they needed the interest they could receive more than anyone, but their lack of knowledge caused them to give the bank a huge gift: the interest-free use of their thousands for many years on end.

ATM Addiction

Automated teller machines (ATMs) are a great invention. They give you convenient access to your cash. That access is free or very modestly priced if you're using your own bank's ATM, but it is much more expensive if you're using another bank's ATM. There is something hypnotic or maybe even addictive about using ATMs. That's the only way I can explain why millions of people spend millions of dollars each year for access to their cash through other banks' ATMs. You can simplify your financial life and save a lot of money if you make yourself the following promise: *I will not develop a habit of using other banks' ATMs.*

Why Credit Cards Aren't an Important Part of Your Banking

Now we come to credit cards. The best way to look at a credit card is as an extension of your checking account. A credit card is a way to pay for something out of your checking account, with a few weeks' delay. If you think of a credit card as anything else, you could be headed for trouble.

Some people, almost by accident, begin to think of a credit card as a way to increase their buying power or even as a way to increase their income. That's not accurate. Actually, it's just a delayed way to pay for something out of checking. So if you don't have the money in checking, don't use the credit card. It's that simple.

Continuing credit card balances are financial poison. On most cards, the interest rate is so high that you'll spend years and thousands of dollars paying them off, if you just make the minimum payments on an average balance. Promise yourself: *I won't keep a balance on my credit card.*

Remember how you sometimes have to trick yourself into doing the right thing? If you're trying to cut back on credit card use and find it difficult, here are some ways to help yourself succeed:

☐ Cut back on the number of cards you have. For any excess card that you won't need, cut up the card and notify the company that you're closing the account.

☐ As soon as you make a charge, find a way to squirrel away that money until the bill comes in. You might deduct it from your checking balance, you might set aside the money in savings—but whatever you do, make yourself aware that the money's spent.

☐ If you're subject to impulse purchases, freeze your credit card inside a Ziploc bag inside a block of ice in the freezer. By the time your card thaws, your impulse purchase fever may have cooled.

Debit Cards

Debit cards look a lot like credit cards, but they have one important difference. When you use a debit card, the money comes straight out of your checking account. With a credit card, you wait until the bill comes before you have to pay.

Since using a debit card is just like writing a check, don't use your debit card unless you know you have the money in checking to cover your purchase. You can save a lot of embarrassment and extra fees if you pay attention to your checking balance.

Debit cards make it easy to fall into bad record-keeping habits. If you just go out and use your debit card without writing down what you spent or saving the receipt, you can easily overdraw your account. On the positive side, using a debit card is quicker and easier than writing a check. Also, you don't have to carry as much cash, which can be lost or stolen.

When you consider the good and bad, debit cards are fine, as long as you remember that the money comes straight out of checking. In fact, if you're uncomfortable with credit cards, you may find a debit card works well for you, giving you most of the benefits of credit cards without running up debt.

Too Many Straws

You and a friend are going to a ball game on a hot, sunny day. On the way your friend buys a small soda and gets five straws to go with it.

"Why?" you ask.

Your friend says, "I want the five straws because I'm going to drink a lot and keep from getting dehydrated!"

We laugh because we understand it's the size of the cup that counts, not the number of straws. Your friend might be able to drink through five straws at once, but that will just empty the cup faster.

Your checking account is that cup. What counts is what's in the cup, not how many ways you can get it out. Today, there are lots of ways to get money out of your checking account. You can get it out by writing a check, of course. You can get it out by using a debit card. You can get it out, with a few weeks' delay, by using a credit card. But none of these ways to get money out will do anything to increase your spending power.

When you see an attractive credit card come-on, remember that it's checking, checking, checking. That's where the money comes from. Do you need another way to get money out of checking? Usually the answer is no. Few people really need as many credit cards as they have.

If you see a credit card promotion and you're tempted to get a card you don't need, go buy yourself a soda. Get five straws and try to drink through them all at once. Go ahead, try it. The result may be funny. Then remember the point and turn down the extra credit card.

If you have chronic difficulty in turning down credit cards, the problem may be deeper than your personal financial strategy. It may result from an excessive desire to have the things of this world. Living in a consumer society as we do, certainly we're all vulnerable to materialism. For that matter, compared with murder, materialism may seem to be a small shortcoming. Still, the Scripture warns, "Do not love the world or anything in the world. If anyone loves the world, the love of the Father is not in him" (1 John 2:15). The corrosive influence of materialism is nothing new, and God wants better for us.

Don't I Get to Have Any Fun?

If you think of it as fun to go out shopping and run up credit card balances without any thought of how to pay for it, all this advice about cutting back on credit will make me seem to be a spoilsport. Trust me, that's not what I'm trying to be.

I have seen financial lives ruined by credit cards. It's no fun dodging bill collectors, collection phone calls and bankruptcy. Even if you don't mind, it's unpleasant and even frightening for those around you. It's far better to have the kind of fun that's unspoiled by worries about how to pay for it.

Group Study Activities and Questions

1. At the end of this chapter you'll find a set of cards that represent the different jobs that might be done at a barn raising. Photocopy them and cut them apart. They'll help your study group realize how great it is that God has given us different abilities, so that we can work as teams more effectively than we could as individuals.

a. Along with everyone in the group, draw a card at random. Then answer this question: Would you be good at doing what your card says?

b. Now trade your card for someone else's—but only if the other party will consent. Answer again: Would you be good at doing what your card says now?

c. Who won and who lost when people traded cards?

d. What would you do at a barn raising if you didn't think you were good at anything on any of the cards?

e. Could house raisings today take the place of home insurance? Why or why not?

2. Do you believe that buying insurance shows a lack of trust in God? Why or why not?

3. If insurance customers choose the lowest deductible possible, they have the smallest out-of-pocket expense when an accident occurs. So isn't it a good idea to get the lowest deductible? Why or why not?

4. Read the parable of the talents (Matthew 25:14-30). Is this parable actually about money? If not, what is it about?

5. Is it possible to have "too much money" in your checking account? To have "too much money for your own good"? Explain.

6. Why would freezing a credit card in a block of ice help some people control their overspending? Couldn't they just thaw it out and go shopping anyway? What else might work for people with a credit problem?

BARN RAISER **Carpenter** Hammering, sawing, nailing	**BARN RAISER** **Gofer** Run various errands
BARN RAISER **Carpenter's** **Helper** Assist carpenter	**BARN RAISER** **Morale Officer** Keep everyone happy
BARN RAISER **Roofer** Build roof support system, roofing	**BARN RAISER** **Child-Care** **Worker** Take care of the kids all day
BARN RAISER **Roofer's Helper** Assist roofer	**BARN RAISER** **Cook** Prepare meals for all workers
BARN RAISER **Electrician** Do all electrical work	**BARN RAISER** **Clean-up** Clean up messes as they occur
BARN RAISER **Building** **Supervisor** Manage construction workers	**BARN RAISER** **Support** **Supervisor** Manage non- construction workers

4

A Roof over
Your Head

There's no place like home.
DOROTHY, in *The Wizard of Oz*

F OR MOST OF US, PAYING FOR THE PLACE where we live is our single largest monthly expense. If we want to worry less about money, this is one expense we need to manage.

The Basic Question: What Do I Need?

Getting the right housing starts with asking the question "What do I need?" Before you answer, consider the difference between needing and wanting. Certainly we should all have the housing we need; everyone needs shelter. Beyond that, if we go for something nicer, then that's a want—to be traded off against all the other wants we may have.

So, how much housing does an individual or a family need? Consider that in Japan it's common for five people to live together in nine hundred square feet of space. Consider that just a generation ago, the average family home in the United States was around one thousand square feet, with two bedrooms and one bathroom. Therefore, if you say that you need more than nine hundred or a thousand square feet, you're probably wrong. You don't need it; you want it. You'll probably get it, too, but at the outset it's important to understand the difference between housing needs and housing wants.

Very few people looking for housing in the United States or Western Europe today are looking to satisfy their needs. Instead, they're looking to satisfy their wants. So when you say, "We really need a fireplace" or "We really need a two-car garage," you're talking about wants and not needs. Young people sometimes add up their "needs" and conclude that their first house must be much grander than the house they grew up in!

Keep in mind also that you don't *need* to buy a home, as opposed to renting. Buying is a want. It's one option, along with renting and leasing. It may be the best option for you, especially if you plan to stay in the same place for more than five years (and if you don't mind the maintenance, lawn care and other obligations that come with owning a home). It may not be the best option at all, especially if you expect to move within a few years.

If you have a goal of home ownership and you're currently renting, there's a lot to be said for continuing to rent for a time while saving money and checking out areas and possibilities for your new home. People sometimes say that rent money is "wasted," but that's not true. You pay rent money in exchange for a place to live, typically less than would be required for you to buy a property. Buying a home too soon can lead to many more problems than would continuing to rent for a time.

In summary, you'll be happier and not as worried if you buy less housing than you can afford. If you do this, you'll be saving on the most difficult kind of cost to manage: a fixed cost. You have to pay for it, month after month after month, no matter how much or how little use you make of it. If you stretch all the way up to buy as much house as you can just barely afford, you'll have to make the payments. You can be in trouble fast if you have unexpected financial setbacks. Remember your built-in happy-o-stat too. You'll feel happier right away when you move into nicer housing, but over time your happy-o-stat will kick in and it won't feel much different from living in something not quite as nice

> We are sometimes asked to consider "What would Jesus do?" In the case of housing, we know what Jesus did. He did not own a home (Matthew 8:20). He apparently did not, however, advise others not to own homes. Simon Peter owned a home that he and others used (Matthew 8:14), and Mary and Martha in Bethany owned a home where Jesus was a welcome guest (Luke 10:38). It is equally clear that Christians are sometimes called on to leave homes or lands for the sake of their faith (Mark 10:29-30; Luke 18:29-30).

Should You Stretch a Little Anyway?

When you're thinking about new housing, you may be encouraged by well-meaning people who are trying to get you to "stretch." Most of the time, it would not be a good idea. Consider some of their arguments:

□ *Your pay will go up over time, making your new house or apartment more affordable.* Probably your pay will go up over time, and so the greatest danger will be shortly after you move in. If you have stretched to try to manage a higher housing payment than is comfortable, you're vulnerable to financial setbacks when you can least afford them. Further, if you're paying rent or a variable-rate mortgage payment, it's entirely possible that your monthly payment will go up as time passes—maybe even faster than your ability to pay.

□ *Real estate is the best investment you can make.* This argument comes from an earlier time when real estate only went up and never went down. Even today it's possible that a house will appreciate in value more than other investments you could make. However, you're already putting a huge amount of money into your house. Good investment principles call for spreading your money around, or diversifying. Even if your house does go up in value, it's difficult to tap in to that value. Typically you have to borrow some of the increased value if you're to get access to it.

□ *You're doing it for your family.* Don't follow this reasoning into over-extending yourself. Your family will enjoy its housing a lot more if you're not worrying about how to meet the rent or the mortgage. Don't throw away mental comfort for creature comfort or status. Whatever you do, don't overextend yourself "for the sake of the kids." Kids are surprisingly unaware of how good or bad their housing is.

□ *The kids need their own rooms.* I have seen families get trapped by the supposed need to have one room per child. Although it's nice, it's certainly not a need. Having one room per child also ill prepares kids for the time when they will need to share quarters with others, such as when they go to college, when they enter volunteer or military service—or, one day, when they get married. Some families have spent a lot of time, effort and money getting separate rooms for their teenagers, just before the teenagers left the nest. Then they were left with too much house. Keep in mind that having one room per child is an extreme rarity in the history of people on earth; today's advanced societies are among the few in earth's history affluent enough to even consider such a use of housing.

You can simplify your life if you resolve to buy less housing than the maximum you can afford. If you find yourself wanting more, consider a small indulgence. Beyond the reasonable amount you're considering spending, think about setting a modest additional budget that you can spend any way you want for nicer housing. New paint and carpet, small carpentry projects and the like can make your house much more pleasant. Within this additional budget, you can indulge, while avoiding a costly move to something altogether different.

For committed Christians, there's another reason to buy less housing than the maximum you can afford. We are called to serve our neighbors and spread the good news (Matthew 28:19; Luke 10:37). Yet we can't be good witnesses to people who live in a state of material comfort far below us. We can't understand their daily lives as well, and they won't be as open to us.

This was pointed out with special force in twentieth-century mission work. When missionaries occupied modern housing while living among profoundly poor people, they found it difficult to connect with those people. The solution was to have missionaries live in substantially the same conditions as the people they were serving. This often meant that the missionary would be someone who grew up in that society and received missionary training, rather than someone who had never been to the country before getting the mission assignment.

Don't Buy in a Hurry

Do whatever it takes to avoid buying a house in a hurry. Many bad things can happen in such a situation, from getting a bad deal to moving into a total disaster of a house.

Sometimes circumstances seem to call for buying a house right away. Most often they involve some variation on the theme "I only want to move once." The reasoning is that if someone doesn't buy a house right away, there will have to be a move to temporary housing, then on to a more permanent location. Moving is a hassle, it's true—but the things that can go wrong when you buy in a hurry are boundless.

Most housing markets are "thin," meaning there are a small number of buyers and sellers in a given year. It's not like buying a car, when you can go and drive everything on the market. Each house is unique, and if you buy in a hurry, you'll have to pick from the tiny fraction of a community's houses that are on sale at any given time.

Not buying in a hurry also means having time to get a home inspection done. Of all the horror stories I have heard in home buying, the great majority of them would have been avoided if the buyers had taken time to do it right, including having a professional tell them just what they were getting.

I have met a lot of people who regretted moving too fast to buy a particular house. I have met very few who felt that they should have moved faster to buy a particular house. Somehow, when the time is right, a home is there.

> The proverbs in the Old Testament were written in a time quite different from our own. Therefore they can't include any specific advice about buying a home in the world of the twenty-first century. However, the proverbs are based on universal truths about people, their behavior and their spiritual condition. They clearly recognize the folly of buying in a hurry: "The plans of the diligent lead to profit as surely as haste leads to poverty" (Proverbs 21:5).

Work with an Attorney

There are many lawyer jokes, and I have sometimes been guilty of telling them (but always in fun). The one place where you don't want to joke around is when you're buying or selling a home. At that point, you need a lawyer, no joke.

If for no other reason than because you need someone to guide you through the paperwork, you should be working with an attorney. At a meeting to sign the papers for a home sale (a "closing"), you'll be called on to place your signature on perhaps dozens of pieces of paper. By signing, you are making certain commitments. Without an attorney, you're making commitments that you might not even understand.

Also consider that you'll be involved in only a few such closings in your lifetime. Real estate attorneys do hundreds of these. They develop experience that can help you stay out of trouble. If there is trouble, they're on the hook and you have someone to hold responsible. For the amount typically charged, it's a bargain.

While You Live There

During the time that you live in a house, you need to keep two main points in mind: maintenance and refinancing.

Unless you're unusually conscientious, don't make perfect maintenance your goal. Instead, try to pay special attention to items that have large future costs if neglected. One good example is a leaking roof. If you see wet places in the ceiling that look like water is getting in somehow, do something right away! Often the problem will just be sealing around a vent pipe or chimney. Caught early, it won't be expensive to fix. Later on, it can mean having to do reroofing and replacement of damaged roof and interior parts. On the other hand, it won't hurt much if it takes you a while to get around to repainting some dull exterior trim.

Make sure that you hang on to the loan papers you sign when you take out a mortgage, and commit yourself to refinancing your loan when interest rates turn in your favor. Promise yourself: *I will refinance the mortgage when the savings outweigh the cost of refinancing. I won't put it off.*

We live in a time when interest rates on home mortgages can change quite a bit, both up and down. When interest rates go down, there's an opportunity to make yourself financially better off—but it's important to take proper advantage of it.

How do you know when to consider refinancing? One rule of thumb is to look into it when interest rates have dropped more than two percentage points. Another rule of thumb is to refinance when your lower monthly payments would pay off the refinancing costs in two years' time. You have to use your common sense though: if interest rates have dropped a lot but you're getting ready to move, you shouldn't refinance. You won't be in the house long enough to recoup the costs.

Here's an example: You have an $800 house payment and interest rates have gone down two percentage points since the time you started paying on that loan. By refinancing, you might save $130 per month. Refinancing will cost you some money, but you'll gain back more than $3,000 in two years with this kind of savings.

Now suppose you expect to stay in the house five more years. It pays you to refinance if the costs are $3,000. You'll have a $130 savings each month, you'll have broken even in two years, and then the $130 savings will continue each month for the life of the loan.

Now, don't blow it! After you scrape the money together and refinance the loan, one possibility is that you'll just spend your new-found $130 monthly savings. You don't have to use it to make the house payment, so it just gets away. Further, if you refinance for the same period as your original mortgage—say, thirty years—you're now further away from paying off the mortgage.

How can you avoid letting the long-term savings of refinancing get away? Here are some possibilities:

☐ Refinance to save that money each month, and have the savings automatically deducted and sent to your SIT fund or an investment account. If you don't see it, you won't be as tempted to spend it. Then that money will go to work for you, earning interest or other investment income.

☐ Refinance to a shorter time period. That is, if you have a thirty-year mortgage at a high interest rate, consider refinancing with a fifteen-year mortgage. It may surprise you how little it costs to cut fifteen years off the end of the mortgage.

☐ Refinance—but instead of saving money on monthly payments, check out a loan schedule that leaves your monthly payment unchanged. After all, if you were paying $800 a month before, you can keep paying $800 a month. But with lower interest rates, that loan will have a shorter term. You'll be putting money away, but painlessly.

Whatever you do, don't sit on a high-interest-rate loan and pay thousands of dollars in unnecessary interest. I have known of people, including some in severe financial straits, who paid more than necessary every month because they never got around to checking out a refinancing option. Although it pays to go slow in purchasing a house, legitimate refinancing is different. Then you know the house and you know the neighborhood. All you're doing is changing the terms of the loan in your favor.

Notice that I referred to "legitimate refinancing," in which you seek out a better mortgage deal. Look out for predatory refinancing, in which an unscrupulous lender seeks you out with a worse deal. The deal may look good, but predatory deals often involve giving you "cash out" or a lower monthly payment in return for a higher debt or a longer term. A good rule here is this: Don't refinance with anyone who found you over the phone.

Compare any unsolicited deal with quotes from reputable local mortgage lenders. There have actually been cases of predatory lenders who refinanced zero-percent loans for low-income families. That's right, these families were getting the best interest deal possible and they were tricked out of it into higher-interest loans. The families were living in housing built by the charitable organization Habitat for Humanity. Unscrupulous lenders hid the true terms of the loans from the families and tricked them into signing. No reputable local mortgage lender would refinance a zero-percent Habitat for Humanity loan!

A Smart Dumb Investment

Some financial writers think it's dumb to reduce mortgage debt or pay off a mortgage sooner or later. They're right, to a point. If you have the ability to pay off a mortgage, or pay it off sooner, then you have at least one good alternative to paying down that debt: leave the debt as it is, and take your money to some investments, where you can get a high return.

There's nothing wrong with this argument except that so many people find it difficult to put extra money into investments. If they were to arrange a high monthly payment that would pay the house off sooner, somehow they'd find a way to make the payment. Or they could find a way to make extra payments on the loan to shorten the mortgage. But if they had that extra money just sitting around in checking, somehow it would leak out of the checkbook. So if you have the discipline to maintain a low, long-term mortgage and use the money you save to invest for the future, fine. If you don't think you have that discipline but do think you'd be able to put away some extra money into retiring a home mortgage, do that. It's a smart dumb investment.

Don't Sell in a Hurry

There always comes the time when you feel that you need to sell a house. Sometimes it's obvious, as when you have accepted a job in another city. Other times it's more a matter of choice, as you consider moving up to a bigger house or a nicer neighborhood. Whatever you do, don't sell in a hurry.

This advice has at least two meanings. The first meaning is that, even when you're sure you need to sell, you shouldn't set artificial time limits—especially very short ones—on how long you're willing to wait. In most times and most parts of the country, you'll short-change yourself if you decide to unload the house in thirty days, period.

The second meaning of the advice not to sell in a hurry is this: you should examine alternatives to selling and moving. If you have just had an argument with your sixteen-year-old about tastes in music and feel you just need more room, consider whether you can hang on until that sixteen-year-old is out of the nest. Or if you truly want a fireplace, check into adding a fireplace to your current house. Or if you feel you simply must have more storage space, look carefully at how you're using your current storage space. Some interior finish contractors can accomplish near-miracles with clever use of existing closets and similar areas.

Notice that the advice isn't "Don't sell"; it's "Don't sell in a hurry." After thinking it over, you may decide that selling and moving is the best choice for you. Fine! You'll now have the satisfaction of knowing you didn't make a hasty decision.

About Real Estate Agents

Dan and Elizabeth put their house up "For Sale by Owner" and sold it that way. William and Jane listed theirs with a real estate agent and sold it that way. Which couple made the right decision? Both did!

Dan and Elizabeth had a house in excellent condition in an area that a small number of home buyers deliberately sought out. They handled the uncomplicated transaction themselves. Although there was inconvenience from the showings and other things, in the end they saved a lot of money.

William and Jane had a house with possible structural problems located in a flood plain, but with an excellent location in a good neighborhood. Their real estate agent coordinated a sale, together with some home inspection and reconstruction that had to be done. He earned his commission on a rather complicated transaction.

If you want to try to sell a house without a real estate agent, get started early and be prepared for some inconvenience. You can save a lot of money in return for what you do. If you later list the house with a real estate agent, you'll be getting much wider exposure and a guiding hand for the details of finishing up the transaction—and that's worth a lot, so much that you might consider starting with the real estate agent in the first place.

It's especially important for first-time buyers and sellers to work with a good real estate agent. How do you find a good one? The best way is to ask around for personal recommendations. This takes some time, but remember, you don't want to buy or sell in a hurry anyway.

Group Study Activities and Questions

1. Consider the immediate family or household of which you are currently a part.

a. What is the minimum number of bedrooms you need?

b. What is the minimum number of bathrooms you need?

c. Do you know of a family or household living in your area that is made up of the same number of people as yours but that occupies a smaller number of bedrooms and bathrooms than you specified? If so, how can they get by with less than they "need"? What does it mean to "need" something if you can get by without it?

2. In your opinion, are people generally happier today than they were in the time of your grandparents? If not, why not? Is it that their housing or food or clothing is worse than in the time of your grandparents?

3. Would Jesus have us (1) live in mansions or (2) live in something less than mansions so that we could identify with others and have more money to give away? Why not small houses instead of large houses, for the same reason? Why not mobile homes or tents instead of small houses? Does Jesus want us to be homeless?

4. What does Proverbs 21:5 say to someone who wants to buy or sell a house in a hurry? Is it possible to take the advice of Proverbs 21:5 too far or too literally?

5. Deuteronomy 15:1 says, "At the end of every seven years you must cancel debts." This was a part of the Old Testament law that had the effect of keeping people out of debt trouble. Some Christians believe that Deuteronomy 15:1 means they should not take out a home loan with a term longer than seven years. Do you agree?

6. At times there are many people who could save $200 per month by refinancing their mortgages at an expense of $2,000. That is, they'd recoup their refinancing expense in about ten months, then be $200 per month better off for years. Yet they don't refinance. Why don't they?

5

Wheels

The people recognize themselves in their commodities;
they find their soul in their automobile, hi-fi set,
split-level home, kitchen equipment.
HERBERT MARCUSE

I T IS SOMETIMES SAID THAT WE HAVE A "love affair with the automobile," and who can deny the comparison? People who manage their money well for years can throw away thousands in a few minutes when car fever strikes. People who carefully shop for the best deal on paper towels may find themselves driving away from a car deal on custom alloy wheels that would eat up fifty years' savings from careful paper towel shopping. Then all too often that new love is tossed aside when a striking new car comes out.

People often end up worrying about their cars too. There are two chief worries: one, that the car will break down and require inconvenient and expensive repairs; and two, that it will be difficult to meet the car payment due each month.

There are some easy ways to reduce both of these worries, as we'll see in this chapter. The goal is to get relatively safe and reliable transportation at a low cost per mile.

Also, it's true that some people aren't bothered by car fever at all. They easily make reasonable and nonemotional decisions about transportation. When they talk to their car-feverish friends, it's like nonsmokers talking to smokers who are trying to quit. They may understand intellectually, but they don't understand emotionally.

Because money spent on cars may derail your journey toward worrying less about finances, this is a good time to have a look at "wheels."

Jesus Christ conducted his earthly ministry at a time when walking was the common mode of transportation. So he walked. He shared the life of those around him; he was "made like his brothers in every way" (Hebrews 2:17).

We can only speculate on what Jesus would have done if different means of transportation had been common at the time of his earthly ministry. It is hard to imagine, however, that showy transportation would have been part of the equation.

Jesus Christ obviously did not address the issues raised by automobiles in a direct way. He did address the more enduring point: that when the cares of this world choke out the Word, it cannot bear fruit. In the parable of the sower (Matthew 13:3-23), some of the seed never had a chance, because it was eaten by birds or fell on unsuitable ground. But among the seed that lasted, some of the plants got choked out by thorns and still didn't bear a crop.

Jesus explained how the parable was about people: "The one who received the seed that fell among the thorns is the man who hears the word, but the worries of this life and the deceitfulness of wealth choke it, making it unfruitful" (Matthew 13:22).

Avoid Big Mistakes: Slow Down

The biggest mistake people make in seeing to their transportation needs is this: not seeing to their transportation needs. They do something else when they think about buying a car. Rather than focusing on how to get around, they try to sharpen their image with a car, heal an old hurt or make a statement

Stop and think a minute about your transportation needs (not your wants; we'll get to those in a minute). Where do you feel that you need to go, with how many people, carrying what cargo? Most often, those transportation needs are quite modest and not difficult to fill with any of a variety of cars and trucks available.

Now, beyond your transportation needs, think about what you want and why you want it. This is a great exercise for people who have already fixated on a particular fast car or a van or a pickup truck or whatever. Sometimes people have narrowed the field too fast—and they won't be satisfied for long if they go out and get the vehicle, seemingly, of their dreams.

All this leads to the most important rule for not making bad deals on vehicles and not worrying about them: Don't buy or lease a car in a hurry. If you move fast, you're likely to get the wrong vehicle or a poor deal on the right vehicle. So slow down and ask yourself the following questions:

☐ Why do I want that fast car? If it has great handling at ninety miles per hour, when will I ever legally or sensibly get to use that capability? Am I just trying to impress some people who won't be very impressed anyway?

☐ Why do I have to make a deal so soon? Some people get stampeded into making a deal on a new vehicle too soon because, as they tell me, "the old one just died." Upon further investigation, it turns out that the old one didn't die—it just needed $200 worth of work. That's not dying. That's an excuse for buying that new car. I have seen people lose—no kidding—hundreds of dollars because they thought they had to make a deal right away.

☐ Why do I want that sport utility vehicle? From time to time, there's a fad for sport utility vehicles or trucks. People like the image of the off-road adventurer, so they buy a vehicle that can climb mountains. Or they like the image of the cowboy, and they claim a part of it by buying a pickup truck. They tell themselves or others they *need* it because, remember, it was hard to get down to the lake on vacation two years ago. But then most sport utility vehicles get used like cars, going back and forth to work and to the grocery store—with unused capabilities and higher operating costs than other vehicles.

Now maybe you want to go beyond transportation the next time you buy a vehicle. Maybe you want to indulge a taste that you've had for some time. If you do, this is a good time to bring in the concept of "bounded frittering." Assign yourself, in advance, a budget that you can fritter away on a vehicle without having to justify it to yourself or anyone. Then stick to your limit. If you spend that bounded frittering on custom wheels or leather seats or a killer sound system, but avoid making a serious mistake like buying a fast sports car you don't need at all, you'll be far better off.

All the while, keep in mind that when you're buying a car in a hurry, you're at the mercy of the seller. If you're lucky, that person will be kind and give you a decent deal despite recognizing that you

From a moral or spiritual point of view, why do you care if you get a bad deal? After all, the money will go to the salesperson and dealership, and maybe they need the money more than you. One reason to care is that if you get a bad deal by buying a car in a hurry, you only encourage future deals to be made in a hurry—perhaps very much to the disadvantage of future customers. On the other hand, if you buy from a fair, low-pressure salesperson, you encourage that kind of dealing in the future.

I heard about a refugee family that spoke very little English. They moved to the United States and, after a few months, went into an automobile dealership and got an extremely bad deal on a new car they didn't need. It's bad enough that they got more car than they needed for more than they could really pay; it's as bad or worse that the salesperson who handled the deal was rewarded for taking advantage of the weak. One who oppresses the poor "shows contempt for their Maker," Proverbs 14:31 tells us. Also, when that sale went the way it did, it didn't reward the ethical and honest dealers and salespeople, who went without a sale that ended up with their less honest competitors.

could be overcharged hundreds or thousands of dollars without protesting. If you're not lucky, well, you'll get a bad deal.

Negotiating a Deal: The Lake Wobegon Effect

Buying a car means negotiating, most of the time. It goes back to the tradition of horse trading, which had a deservedly poor reputation.

I am constantly amazed at the number of people who think they're good negotiators. They think they'll get the best of the deal when they bargain with an automobile dealer. Ask yourself: *What do I do best?* Usually it's a skill that you use on your job every day. If you're a carpenter, you're good at being a carpenter. What do you think would happen if an auto salesperson strapped on a tool belt once every few years and climbed up on a ladder to drive a few nails? Would that person be better at it than you, someone who practices it every working day? Of course not! Then why do so many people think that they can out-negotiate someone who negotiates every day for a living?

People are subject to something called "the Lake Wobegon Effect," named by the humorist Garrison Keillor. Keillor said that at his fictional Lake Wobegon all the children are above average. Mathematically that's impossible, since the average defines the middle, but that's what the people of Lake Wobegon thought. And for some reason, in their minds, most people believe they are above average at negotiating for a new car. Most of them are wrong. Most are about average, an important number are below average, and a few are excellent negotiators—usually people who practice it in their line of work.

As a university professor, I had the chance to check this idea out when I supervised a student's senior project. The student, Grant Furick, found in a random survey that more than half the people think they're better-than-average negotiators. They're not all correct. They can't be.

How to Get a Good Deal Anyway

How, then, can the average buyer get a good deal anyway? The most important rule is to slow down. Time is on your side. Rarely will you get the best deal right up front.

Remember how "the perfect is the enemy of the good"? That applies with special force in buying a car. A "good" deal in this case is a deal at a so-called one-price or no-haggle dealer. These are dealers who say up front that they're going to post their best price and then not negotiate with you. Their announced, prediscounted price is supposed to represent an average deal that someone with average negotiating ability would get, if that person had negotiated prices.

I have seen people pass up a no-haggle deal to negotiate at another dealer and come out with a much worse deal. In their case, the perfect was the enemy of the good. By trying to negotiate the very best deal, they went through a stressful situation and ended up with a bad deal. Mercifully, some of them never found out what a bad deal they got.

One of my friends had this happen to her. After the deal was over, she came around to tell me what a good price she had been able to negotiate. She knew it was a good price, she said, because the manager "told me what a good deal I had gotten." I didn't ask her to consider the manager's motivation and truthfulness!

You can read about elaborate strategies for getting a good deal in magazines like *Consumer Reports*. Those strategies work by starting from a good estimate of dealer cost and then negotiating up from the cost (instead of down from the artificially inflated asking price). For many people, they're too much bother. Therefore, if you can't or won't follow a systematic negotiating strategy starting from dealer cost, make sure that you don't get in a hurry. Shop around, check the one-price dealers and delay your final decision. Typically, the deals will get better, not worse.

There's a saying among car dealers that 80 percent of the profit comes from 20 percent of the customers. Don't be in that 20 percent. If you shop more carefully, you'll be encouraging ethical and honest behavior.

Simplifying by Buying Used

It simplifies things a lot to decide in advance that you're going to buy a used car, not a new one. Remember that you can *buy* a new car but you can't *own* a new car. Why? Because once you drive it off the dealer's lot, you own a used car. In every way that counts, that car is now used. The only question is whether to get a newer used car or an older used car.

Part of my past research has been on new and used car pricing. In that research I found that the best deal, if you can afford it, is on a relatively new used car. These cars, referred to as "nearly new" or "program" cars, will offer very nearly the service and reliability of a new car. Many will have a substantial amount of the original warranty left.

However, since the initial depreciation of value occurred when the car was driven off the dealer's lot, you get this service and reliability at a substantially reduced cost. Also in your favor is the variety of sources for these cars. If you just have to have a new Ford, your Ford dealer is the only source. If you were to consider a used car, then your possible sources include new car dealers, used car dealers, "superstores" and anyone else who's selling, including private parties in the classified advertisements.

To be sure, there are cases in which a new car is the right choice—for example, if someone has a particular need that could only be met by a difficult-to-find car. We all know the attraction of buying a new car just the way you want it, too, without having to search for a used one with just the right options. I have even had someone ask me, "If everyone buys a used car, then who will buy the new cars that become used cars?" For one thing, I'm not worried about having so much influence that people will altogether stop buying new cars. Car fever is just too strong. But more importantly, if people did turn to used cars in sufficiently large numbers, that would lower the demand for new cars. Eventually the auto industry might end up pricing new cars so that they were more affordable, and then personal finance writers like me could widely recommend them again.

Keep It Simple

The trade is separate. Sometimes people get a relatively good deal negotiating on a new car but then in essence give away their old car to the dealer. The most important simplifying rule here is to keep the "trade" a separate transaction. In fact, you're not making a trade at all; you're buying a car and selling a car. What you think of as your "trade-in" is actually a car you're selling.

You can get an approximate idea of what your car is worth by consulting used car price guides. Banks will often let you have a look at the "gold book" put out by the National Automobile Dealers' Association. There's also a consumer version of the gold book. With Internet access, you can get a variety of estimates on what your car might be worth. More importantly to you, there are increasingly a number of dealers who will quote you a firm price on your car to buy it from you, with or without a purchase of another car from them. These quotes are more important than numbers from price guides, which at best are approximate.

Condition is everything when it comes to valuing used cars, so make sure you have cleaned the car well and done any needed minor repairs before you get quotes on it. Keep in mind that a bad car won't be worth even the lower quotes in the price guides, while a near-perfect one may bring more than even the highest quotes in the price guides. The price guides are only approximate. Still, they can help you avoid "giving away" your car in a trade.

Loans and insurance are separate. The impulse to make a deal on a car and go is powerful. If you have made a good deal on the price of the car, don't let your good deal vanish with a bad deal on financing and insurance. The rule is this: Don't buy insurance or car financing in a hurry. Time is on your side here, just as in the main transaction of buying the car. You'll need time to shop around for the best deals on financing and insurance. Sometimes they will be available through the dealer, but often they won't be. You have to seek out the best deals.

You Probably Shouldn't Lease a Car

Even before you have decided on the car, you should be thinking about financing. In working with people, I have developed a rule of thumb. It's not exactly right for everybody, but it is a good rule: Don't buy a car if it takes you longer than three years to pay for it.

If it takes you longer than three years to pay for it, you probably can't afford it. Here are some of the circumstances this rule can help you avoid:

☐ *Being "upside down."* When you owe more on a car than it's worth, you're "upside down," as they say in the business. That's a bad place to be. If you own a car that's worth $8,000 but you owe $10,000 on it and it gets totaled in an accident, you owe the finance company $10,000, not $8,000. Even when insurance covers the $8,000, you're $2,000 out of pocket. Being upside down is common near the beginning of a long auto loan. You're upside down much less of the time if you limit that loan to thirty-six months.

☐ *Buying "too much car."* Since even very modest cars provide all the transportation most people actually need, how can you limit your spending? Decide in advance that you'll finance it for only thirty-six months, and look for something else if those payments are too high. That's one good way to limit your spending. You have to stick to your guns on this, though. At a car showroom, there's a strong tendency to look only at the monthly loan payment and to forget the fact that the loan might go sixty months (five years!) or more.

☐ *Getting onto the lease merry-go-round.* Car salespeople can make a lease sound good. If you can't afford to buy what you want on thirty-six-month payments, why not go for a thirty-six-month lease? Leases can actually be a good idea—but for most people they're not. When you lease a car, you're just renting it. When the lease term is over, you don't own anything. You have to buy the car then if you want to keep it, so you haven't paid for it in thirty-six months. Often people lease in order to get more car, but it's too much car in the sense that it's more than they can afford. The other problem is that after they lease, people get onto the lease merry-go-round. Having leased for a number of months, and not owning a car at lease's end, they just get into another lease right away. From then on, they never own a car; they just keep leasing ("renting").

Sometimes car manufacturers come out with such good lease terms that people say they "just can't turn it down." It is true that sometimes manufacturers throw their promotional money into leases. When that's true, there's a way of taking advantage of this without getting onto the lease merry-go-round. Just take the figure called the "residual value," the value of the car at the end of the lease. Decide that you'll save up at least that amount by the time the lease is over. One simple way to make sure it happens is to divide that residual value by the number of monthly lease payments, then set aside that amount—faithfully, every month!—into your SIT fund. Then at the end of the lease, you'll be able to buy the car and you'll own it just as if you had financed it over thirty-six months.

What if you can only afford a junker using this rule? What if you don't like the cars that you could afford on thirty-six-month financing? Be careful, and make sure you're not falling into the trap of overestimating your automotive needs. The reliability and durability of cars has improved so much that there are plenty of old cars out there with a lot of life left. Make sure you're not calling the car a "junker" because of styling.

Maintaining a Car

The perfect way of maintaining a car is to do all the recommended service in the owner's manual, on time and only at the authorized dealer. But perfect maintenance isn't a realistic goal for most people. If you put off getting your car maintained because you don't want the bother or expense of doing perfect maintenance, you're doing yourself a big disservice. Cars do hold up better with proper maintenance. Remember the commercial that had a sad mechanic saying, "You can pay me now or pay me later"? It really is true. Preventive maintenance works.

Therefore, if you're tempted to just keep driving that car without maintaining it, make yourself this promise: *I will get the oil changed on schedule, and I will keep all safety items up to date.* Then fix other things as they break. It's not the perfect maintenance plan, but it's way ahead of doing nothing.

Our cars are part of a busy lifestyle, perhaps too busy. Sometimes we get so caught up in our busy lives that we act as if "someone" is doing this to us. In fact, our busy lives result by and large from our own choices. If we choose to do too much, we pay the costs in a lack of time. We don't have the time to spend with those we love, the time to think deeply, the time to pray, the time to appreciate the creation around us.

In his brief time on earth, Jesus Christ had much to do. Yet he took time to pray (Mark 1:35); it was his source of strength. Sometimes when we think we're making decisions on cars, in fact we're making decisions on lifestyles. Let us resolve to get our lifestyles right first—and then arrange for the transportation that fits the chosen lifestyle. An old proverb says that if you give a man a hammer, pretty soon all his problems start to look like nails. If we give ourselves a fancy car with full electronics and a wireless phone, pretty soon all our problems look like they can be solved by dashing from here to there listening to the radio, talking on the phone and going through the drive-through for fast food.

Group Study Activities and Questions

1. Mark a piece of paper with a response to the following question: Relative to the group of people in this room, are you (a) a better-than-average negotiator, (b) a worse-than-average negotiator or (c) an average negotiator?

a. Tally the responses for your group. Did more than half of the people say they're better than average? If so, they can't be right.

b. How do people become good negotiators? Is it a skill that improves with practice? Is it a skill that some people are just born with?

c. How do you know if you got a good deal when you negotiated the price of a new car? If the sales manager of the dealership says you did, is that good evidence that you got a good deal?

d. Can a Christian be a good negotiator in a car showroom?

2. Social observers have said that the United States has "a love affair with the automobile." Do you have a love affair with your automobile? Do you have a love affair with an auto-supported lifestyle?

3. Read the parable of the sower (Matthew 13:3-23). What are the "thorns" that choke out God's Word today? That is, what did Jesus mean when he referred to "the worries of this life and the deceitfulness of wealth"?

4. Many people work hard to save a few cents by buying generic food items, or drive a few miles to save a dollar on gasoline, but then easily agree to automotive options that cost hundreds or thousands of dollars. Why?

5. Do you always have all the recommended maintenance done on your car, and on time? Or do you just drive it until it breaks down? Or something in between? Is it poor stewardship of a resource to do less than all the recommended maintenance? What spiritual attitude is reflected by driving a car with defective safety equipment (bald tires, for example)?

6. Many of us think of our cars as necessary to live our busy lifestyles, and we often think our time is overcommitted. Who made us too busy, and who overcommitted us? Is this even a fair question to ask?

6

The Simple Approach to Investing

*In investing money, the amount of interest you want
should depend on whether you want to eat well or sleep well.*
J. KENFIELD MORLEY

NOW THAT YOU'VE GOTTEN CONTROL of your budget, gotten
your banking and insurance in order, and taken care of housing and
transportation, you're ready for investment. Investment is commit-
ting funds now in hope of a future return. In this chapter we'll have
a look at the basic approach to take with all your investments. Then
in future chapters we'll apply this approach to the different ways
you can invest.

Investment decisions can be a major strain in any marriage or
partnership. Thousands of dollars can sometimes ride on the out-
come. That's just one reason why it's important to give up greed.

There was a time when "Greed is good" showed up as a slogan in
popular culture. That's wrong. In investment you'll find that greed is
bad. Beyond that, greed is counterproductive. In this chapter we'll

see how those who give up greed and forsake the goal of trying to make more money than others actually end up making more money than others.

Giving Up Greed to Make More Money

The strategy I'll show you involves precommitting yourself to the following pledge: "I pledge that I will seek only an average return. I will not be envious when I hear of others who made a killing, and I will not gloat when I hear of others who lost money."

How does it work? And how can people with little investment knowledge get started?

In the area of investment the whole process gets started when you recognize your limitations and stop worrying. You admit that you can't play the stock market. You have a life to live; you can't be checking the stock market every ten minutes. You recognize that you can't win the game of trading stocks all day long against professionals who do it for a living. But that's not bad. You will almost certainly do better by following the strategy of this chapter than you will by playing the game of stock trading. You will likely do better than friends or neighbors who have individual stocks.

In my role as a university professor and director of a center for economic education, I'm often asked, "How can I get started in investing? What stock should I buy?" For most people, the answer is not to buy a stock at all but to buy particular kinds of mutual funds. When you understand the power of mutual funds, you will wonder why so many people settle for the inferior returns of other investments.

For many people, the biggest obstacle to investing is lack of knowledge. They think they have to become experts on the stock market to do well. That's not true. The most expert people in the stock market do well, and those who follow the simple strategy I'll outline do well. The people who do the worst in the stock market are those who think they know the market but don't. Millions of people are in this last category.

Covet is a fine and rare word in the English language. How many times do we hear it used in ordinary speech? The dictionary says it means "to wish for enviously" or "to desire what belongs to another." Covetousness is a sin specifically condemned by the last of the Ten Commandments (Exodus 20:17).

If we start an investment plan to try to make more money than our neighbor, or if we get envious when we hear of a friend's stock market success, then we're coveting. Investment is one of those activities where doing the right thing spiritually (that is, not coveting) has additional, material rewards. In fact, we'll see that most of those who try to make more money than their neighbor end up making less.

To covet is to admit a corrosive spiritual influence into our lives. Our Creator's commandments leave no room for doubt on this.

How to Start: Emergency Cash in a Money Market Fund

The best way for most people to start an investment program is with emergency cash (a SIT fund) stored in a money market account. Remember, "SIT" stands for "surprises, insurance and taxes." Remember too that a money market account allows you easy access to saved money but often pays twice the interest of a bank savings account. Here are the advantages of starting your investment plan with a money market account:

☐ A money market fund is easy to understand. You keep your money there, you earn your share of interest on the assets held by the fund and for all practical purposes your account is like a bank account.

☐ A money market fund introduces you to the world of investing with very little risk. Except under extraordinary circumstances, your money will not lose value but will grow. You'll find that investment firms must make full and sometimes scary disclosures of even remote possibilities. So the official papers for your money market fund will warn you about the fact that your money market account is not as secure as a bank deposit. Of course, the interest is higher, partly as compensation.

☐ You'll have some easy success. You'll see your balance grow a little from quarter to quarter. This is in sharp contrast to some other kinds of investments, in which you have to get used to the idea that they could have sharp swings in value. (Shortly after buying those investments, you can easily see your account worth less than the money you invested.)

☐ You'll establish a relationship with an investment company. You'll be on their account list and begin to get their mailings. Investment will become a less foreign concept to you.

☐ Perhaps most importantly, you'll build up an emergency reserve. Then, as you expand your investments, you won't have to pull your money out to meet unexpected bills. You'll just use your emergency reserve. We'll see that leaving invested money alone is a powerful and important strategy. With your emergency reserve built up, you can draw on it, if necessary, and leave your other investments alone.

Your money market fund account is like a big "super checking" account. It provides a higher return than your bank accounts, but you don't write everyday checks on it.

When is the emergency fund big enough? One good rule is to work toward having three months' pay saved up. You might want more or less, depending on your circumstances, but three months' pay is a good guideline.

If you believe that you could never save up three months' pay, then it's time to go back to the chapter on budgeting. To make any financial progress at all, you have to spend less than you make. There are lots of ways to do that, but here's just one more: The next time you get an income tax refund, give yourself something nice from that money (a meal out or a small frivolous purchase) and use the rest to open a money market account. Or if it's not enough to open a money market account, put it into a bank savings account that you have specifically for the purpose of one day opening a money market account. You'll be glad you did.

You need to understand one important fact about a money market fund: you will not make a killing. You will not see big increases in the value of your fund to brag about. But you will have established the basis of a sound investment program.

About Mutual Funds

If you set out to buy financial assets like stocks and bonds on your own, you'll face a lot of expenses like commissions and sales fees. Especially for small investors, this is why mutual funds make so much sense. When you send your money to a mutual fund, the fund pools your money with that of many other investors and then buys financial assets. You share in the gains and losses of the fund according to how much money you have put in.

A money market fund is a special kind of mutual fund. It invests only in very safe securities, which is part of why it's the ideal way to begin an investment plan.

Stock mutual funds are much more common. Remember that when anyone buys stock, it amounts to buying part ownership of a company. If you own one share of a big corporation and it has 200 million shares of stock outstanding, then your part ownership is very small. It's one 200-millionth, to be exact. You then have a claim on one 200-millionth of the company's profits, some of which will be reinvested and some of which will be paid out to you as a dividend.

It would be possible for you to buy different stocks, hold them in hopes that they will grow, and collect the dividends on your investment. It's much better, though, for most investors to hold stock through mutual funds. The mutual fund holds on to the stock, collects the dividends and passes through the resulting income to those who have invested in the mutual fund.

Most mutual funds are actively managed, meaning that their managers try to pick stocks that will do better than the general run of stocks, or "beat the market." It's costly to hire analysts and trade frequently, trying to beat the market. How do they know when they have succeeded? They calculate how well their fund did, then compare that with how well the market did.

Indexes and Index Funds

To calculate how well the market did, analysts use stock market indexes. An index is just a collection of stocks. Indexes are averaged using different methods, but the intent is the same: to indicate how the market is doing.

For example, the Dow Jones Industrial Average is an index made up of thirty stocks. The performance of the Dow Jones is widely reported and you can easily calculate whether you're "beating the Dow." You could make your own holdings duplicate the performance of the Dow Jones by buying small amounts of the thirty stocks in the Dow, in the same proportion they're present in the Dow. But of course, there would be a lot of time, expense and hassle for a small investor in owning those thirty stocks.

The Standard & Poor's 500 is a collection of five hundred big stocks originally tracked by the firm called Standard & Poor's, now a division of the publisher McGraw-Hill. You could duplicate the performance of the Standard & Poor's 500 by buying small amounts of those five hundred stocks in the right proportions—but you'd have to pay the fees and commissions of five hundred different stock transactions! That would be impractical for a small investor.

This is where an index fund comes in. As a special kind of mutual fund, it pools funds from you and other investors, then invests the money in the stocks that make up an index. Because it has millions of dollars to deal with, it avoids the high commissions and fees that an individual investor would face. Better yet, it can easily invest in five hundred or more stocks.

So if you invest in a Standard & Poor's 500 index fund, you'll get something like the average return of those five hundred stocks. Some will do well, some will do poorly, and you'll get the average. What's so good about that?

The Grand Strategy: Buy and Hold Index Funds

What's so good about getting the average return is that, over time, the average return of the stock market is very attractive. If you only get that average return—and you do it without worrying—you're ahead of the game. The average return in the stock market over the past sixty years has been enough to double your money every six or seven years, then double again in another six or seven years. So getting the average return is quite good.

In an important sense you'll do even better than the average. Here's why: what matters to you is the net return on your money, after all expenses have been subtracted. Think about a mutual fund that starts out making large returns (a high gross return) but has to spend a lot of your money doing it. That fund would have a low net return after all those expenses were subtracted. As it turns out, it's expensive to try to beat the market. When mutual funds try, they hire high-priced analysts and spend a lot of time and effort trading to get high returns.

On the other hand, index funds face none of the expenses of trying to beat the market, since they have given up that goal in advance. They get average returns. But they get those average returns at below-average costs, so you get to keep more of the money your investment earned.

Sometimes those funds that try to beat the market do well. Their managers spot good stocks, buy them and hold on to them long enough for superior returns. Still, they incur expenses in doing this.

In most years these funds don't do well enough to outperform the indexes. The *Wall Street Journal* of May 12, 1998, quoted a leading analytical service as reporting that over a ten-year period an astounding 86 percent of diversified U.S. stock funds lagged behind the Standard & Poor's 500 Index.*

No matter how many times I write and speak about these facts, I still can't get over them. A majority of funds trying to beat the market don't end up beating the market at all. You'd be better off if you could buy a little bit of all the stocks out there—and that's what, in effect, you do with an index fund.

There are some technical reasons why the 86 percent figure is a little exaggerated, but the basic truth remains: in most years actively managed mutual funds do not beat index funds. Figure 6.1 displays publicly available data showing how often a total stock market index fund would beat the average comparable mutual fund.

1991	1992	1993	1994	1995	1996	1997	1998	1999	2000
56%	53%	44%	59%	77%	59%	77%	70%	58%	25%

Figure 6.1. Percentage of mutual funds outperformed by stock market index

In this ten-year period there were eight years in which the index fund investor would have done better than the average investor in an actively managed fund. There were only two years in which the index fund investor would have done worse. But more importantly, the index fund investor gets these high returns without doing research on investment strategy and without worrying about whether a mutual fund's management will change.

Don't just take my word for it. If you have some library time, check out John Bogle's *Common Sense on Mutual Funds* or Burton Malkiel's *A Random Walk down Wall Street*. If you have even more time, look up the references in the back of Malkiel's book. Or do an

---

*Jonathan Clements, "The Truth Investors Don't Want to Hear on Index Funds and Market Soothsayers," *Wall Street Journal*, May 12, 1998, p. C1.

Internet search on "index funds vs. actively managed funds." Or seek out any information source that's not paid for by people selling actively managed funds (that's important). You will find that index funds have an impressive record.

Typically, the more people know about the stock market, the more impressed they are with the merits of index funds. I'm an advocate of index fund investing. I earned a Ph.D. in economics in 1980 and have seen the evidence in favor of index funds pile up every year since then. Don't take my word for it, though; people a lot smarter than I am are index fund investors, including William F. Sharpe, Stanford University finance professor and Nobel laureate in economics.

People who know less about financial markets are likely to underestimate the advantages of indexing. It's hard to call index fund investing a secret, but it's surprising how many people get inferior returns each year because they do something worse than index fund investing.

In economics there's a wise saying that goes, "There's no such thing as a free lunch." When something good is offered to you, there's often a tradeoff or hidden cost. Are index funds a free lunch? No, not at all. You give up the possibility of getting the truly meteoric returns that would come from picking a hot stock or a hot fund at the right time. And why do I and other analysts think that's all right? Because in return for giving up the highest possible returns, you eliminate the risk of the worst possible returns. You get an assurance that you'll do about average—and that in a market where the average is very good.

There's one more important part of the formula called "buy and hold index funds." It's the "buy and hold" part (as opposed to "buy and sell"). Over periods of years, the stock market shows impressive returns. Over shorter periods, the returns can be low, negative or strongly negative. You can lose a lot by buying and selling in these short periods. That's the point of having your emergency fund set up. Your objective is to buy and hold.

 This is probably a good place to remind ourselves of why we want a high return on our investment over time. We want that high return so that we can achieve our prayerfully decided financial objectives. We want that high return so that we can care for our families, give money away, live comfortably, educate the next generation—the reasons could go on and on. The object is not to get a high return so that we can impress ourselves with our own importance or, worse yet, claim independence from God.

All that we have we owe to God. One psalmist wrote, "The earth is the LORD's, and everything in it, the world, and all who live in it" (Psalm 24:1). Without that reminder, we run the danger of falling into the error of the rich fool.

The subject of a parable of Jesus, a rich man had such a good crop one year that he didn't have enough room to store it all. He planned to tear down his barns, build more for his possessions and then eat, drink and be merry. "But God said to him, 'You fool! This very night your life will be demanded from you. Then who will get what you have prepared for yourself?'" (Luke 12:20). I know a Christian woman who says, "Bigger barns!" when her husband talks about all the money they have made in the market. It's a sobering reminder of what happens when we store up things but are not "rich toward God" (verse 21).

Group Study Activities and Questions

1. On a piece of paper, write down (anonymously) something nice that a neighbor of yours has, such as a new boat or a big-screen television. Then hand in your piece of paper to the group leader, who will record all of the responses on a chalkboard or flip chart. As you consider the list, answer these questions:

a. Is it coveting to admire the nice thing that your neighbor has?

b. Are there any items on the list that would cause more of a problem for you than others would? Are there any items that aren't any problem at all—

because you're glad your neighbor has it but you don't want it?

c. Is it coveting to wish that you had made the same lucrative investment your neighbor made?

d. Are there times in your life when you're more susceptible to wanting something that your neighbor has?

2. What do you usually do with your income tax refund? Would it be difficult to allow yourself a small amount from it to spend on anything you wanted, then save the rest? Why or why not?

3. Do you pay any attention to the day-by-day reports on how the Dow Jones Industrial Average is doing? If that average is much higher or lower in a given day, will that be a topic of conversation among your friends and associates? Will you be emotionally affected by it?

4. Suppose a mysterious stranger walked up and gave you $1,000. It's yours to keep, but the stranger offers you a deal. (You trust her to deal honestly.) She'll flip a coin, and if it comes up heads, you double your money to $2,000. If it comes up tails, you have to give back the $1,000. Would you accept this deal? Would your answer change if the stranger offered you $10,000 for heads and the same deal on tails? What do your answers say about your willingness to take risk?

5. Suppose you learned that your closest friend had turned a $1,000 investment into $20,000 by purchasing the stock of a new bank in town. At the time the friend bought the stock, you didn't hear anything about it. Would you be angry at your friend for not letting you in on the deal? Why or why not? If your friend had risked $1,000 on a speculative investment and lost it all, do you think you would hear about it?

6. Read the parable of the rich fool (Luke 12:16-21). What kinds of "crops" do we harvest today that would raise the possibility that we would fall into the same mistake as the rich fool? Does this parable argue against Christians having savings accounts?

7

Taxes & Other Leakages

In this world nothing can be said to be certain,
except death and taxes.
BENJAMIN FRANKLIN

Benjamin Franklin was right about the inevitability of taxes. Be assured that your money won't escape taxation. There are ways, however, to legally minimize the amount of tax you pay, and we'll have a look at a few of them in this chapter. There's an immediate and self-interested reason why most of us want to minimize the taxes we pay: so we'll have more money for ourselves. There are reasons of principle not to want to pay more than the necessary amount of tax too. And when we look at what happens to invested money, there's reason to think carefully about what we're supporting with our investments.

In the last chapter we saw how to worry less about investments by deciding to buy and hold index funds as an investment strategy. The "buy and hold" part means just that: you hang on to your investments rather than switching them in and out of assets according to the latest fad. The "index funds" part means that, instead of holding individual stocks or something else, you in effect buy a little bit of every stock. You eliminate the anxiety of worrying about how any one company, or even a large group of companies, will do. My favorite stock fund tracks the performance of five thousand stocks. By holding that fund, I deliberately stay away from risking large amounts of money on any given sector of the economy.

It takes a while for the strategy of buying and holding index funds to sink in. We'll explore the strategy in more detail in the next few chapters, and we begin by looking at "leakages," the money that inevitably leaks out of your investments. Money lost to taxes is the most obvious of these.

The Compound Effect of Taxation

If you're not wealthy, you may think that taxation has little effect on your investments—but you're probably wrong. Consider the case of Pat, a young worker who begins saving at age twenty-five for retirement at age sixty-five. Pat works hard and invests $2,000 per year. It makes a tremendous difference whether Pat saves in a taxable or nontaxable way:

☐ If Pat saves in a nontaxable way and receives a long-term return of 10 percent, she retires as a millionaire. Her holdings are worth more than $1.1 million.

☐ If Pat has to pay taxes on investment earnings, Pat will see that possible $1.1 million at age sixty-five shrink to about $500,000 to $700,000. The exact amount depends on her tax situation, but the effect is big in any case.

Why do taxes make so much of a difference? It has to do with the way that growth compounds over time. Ask yourself: *If I had $100 and it grew at 10 percent over time, how long would it take for it to dou-*

ble? *That is, how long until it grew to $200?* A lot of people guess ten years, which sounds reasonable at first. Ten percent of $100 is $10, and so in ten years you'd have collected another $100. That would make the original $100 double.

Although a lot of people guess ten years, their guess is wrong. The answer is more like seven years. After one year, the $100 has grown to $110, it's true. But in the next year, all of that $110 has grown by 10 percent. The whole sum is now worth not $120 but $121. That dollar may seem like a small amount, but over time it adds up. By the end of year three, the original $100 has grown to $133, not $130. The divergence gets greater and greater over time, so that the original $100 doubles in around seven years— when our first guess might have been that it would only be around $170 then.

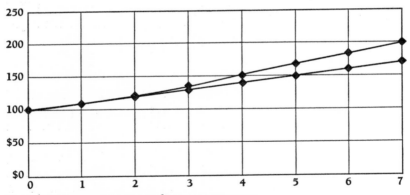

Figure 7.1. Ten percent compounding over seven years

Figure 7.1 shows how $100 growing at 10 percent for seven years actually doubles, rather than just reaching $170, as might be expected. Figure 7.2 shows how the upward curve becomes even more pronounced over long time periods, as the return compounds. In fact, $1,000 left alone to grow at 10 percent becomes more than $45,000 in forty years.

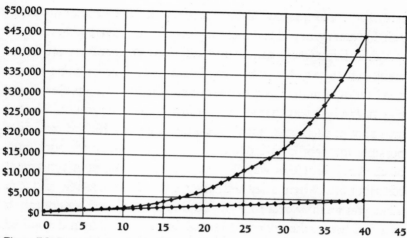

Figure 7.2. Ten percent compounding over forty years

Taxes make the difference between Pat becoming and not becoming a retirement millionaire. This is why I advise people to be very careful about taxes. If Pat saves without looking into the tax angle, that could be a half-million dollar mistake!

Some Christians are uneasy about the idea of saving lots of money for retirement. It's easy to see why. Our emphasis and focus should be on serving God today, and we must avoid the idea that we slave hard all our lives, reserving any happiness for retirement time. God wants us to live joyfully today.

It's also true that we don't want to be a burden on others in retirement, and that argues in favor of saving and investing for that time. So while we should make provisions for retirement, this should not be the only goal of our financial plan.

Some people aren't happy about saving today for retirement. That's understandable. We feel that we have needs for our money today, and retirement seems awfully remote to someone who hasn't yet turned thirty. However, the power of compounding means that we get a lot of future income for a small amount of saving today. The power of compounding tax-free means that we get even more return for saving today. Also, money saved for retirement is available for emergency use, depending on how it's saved.

What if you know all this and still don't want to save for retirement, but instead for something like a first home or some education? Oddly enough, a retirement account with its tax-free status may be the best way to save for that first home or education. The tax laws change each year, but there's a definite trend toward making it possible for people to tap retirement contributions for such purposes. Look at it this way: If you end up leaving your retirement contributions where they are, they compound tax-free and can make you wealthy over time. If you do take them out for education or a first home, the tax consequences are no worse than if you had saved in a nonretirement account anyway.

I deliberately chose the number $2,000 in the example of Pat because that's the amount that taxpayers have long been able to put each year into something known as a "Roth IRA." (Recent changes in the law have raised those limits, but $2,000 is a reasonable goal for many people.) Pat's example is entirely realistic. Ten percent is a reasonable long-term assumption for someone who decides to buy and hold index funds. If Pat is paid weekly, saving less than $40 per paycheck and putting it away can make Pat a retirement millionaire!

Employer-Sponsored Plans

When you understand the effects of taxation, you begin to appreciate the benefits of tax-advantaged ways of saving and investing. Some of the best deals around are sponsored by employers. These plans are known by the sections of the laws that created them, such as 401(k) and 403(b).

The movement in retirement plans is toward more self-direction. You're more in charge of your retirement money, for better or for worse. This is in contrast to older so-called defined benefit plans, in which you would have money taken out of your paycheck while you worked, then receive money after retirement—and all that without having to make many decisions at all. If you have a 401(k) or similar plan, things are different. You have to make decisions about how much to contribute and where to direct the money.

The great thing about many 401(k) and similar plans is that employers match contributions. If you have a 50 percent match, the employer puts in fifty cents for every dollar you invest, and that's like getting an immediate 50 percent return. If you have such a plan where you work, by all means take full advantage of it.

What to Do with Invested Retirement Money

It's understandable that some people feel overwhelmed with the complexity of managing a retirement account. Those accounts generate a lot of paperwork that comes in the mail and isn't always easy to understand. So, what strategy should someone use?

The best long-term strategy is still to buy and hold index funds. The history of asset markets shows that the only people who didn't do well in the long term were those who traded in and out or who held the wrong assets. Your retirement fund is not to be gambled with. Playing financial markets for short-term gain is nothing more than gambling.

Trouble is, many 401(k) and other self-directed retirement plans don't offer index funds as a possible investment choice. If that's true of your self-directed retirement plan, then find the closest thing you can to an index fund. That will usually mean broad-based stock mutual funds. Look over the information on your plan to see which funds hold large numbers of stocks from a variety of sectors of the economy. That's what you want.

These stock funds will usually be actively managed, in that they'll be funds that hire managers who try to pick stocks that will beat the market. Over time, they probably *won't* beat the market, and they'll use up some of your potential return trying. On the bright side, they probably won't underperform the market by much either. Mathematically, any holding of many stocks from a variety of sectors is likely to come fairly close to the market return.

Meanwhile, when you have the opportunity, ask your retirement plan administrators about getting index funds offered in the future.

Your Own Company's Stock

If you work for a corporation, often you have the opportunity to buy its stock on favorable terms. This is usually a good deal, and it may help you identify with your employer to have a stake in the company's ownership.

Still, you should be aware of the risk that you're taking when you hold large amounts of your company's stock. Some of this risk is the same risk that comes from holding any one company's stock. The fortunes of any one company could easily change, dragging down the value of its stock and depressing all the future dividends you might have hoped for. IBM is a great company, and if I worked for that company, I'd love to have a lot of IBM stock—but if I did, I'd be looking for ways to sell it and put the proceeds into index funds.

Even beyond the risk that comes from holding any one company's stock, there's an additional risk that you take when you hold the stock of your employer. If your company goes through bad times, you're more likely to be laid off or at least suffer a loss of income as the company tightens its belt. At the very time your finances suffer because of the company's problems, its stock will also likely be down. It would be far better then to be holding an index fund—holding in effect a little piece of lots of companies from across the economy.

It may seem disloyal, but these are good reasons not to keep a large part of your long-term investments in the stock of the same company that you work for.

Your Nonretirement Funds

Clearly the tax-advantaged ways of investing, like employer-sponsored plans and Roth IRAs, are important for your long-term financial security. There are many years for the advantages to compound and work in your favor.

After taking advantage of these long-term opportunities, you'll want to think about saving and investing for more immediate goals, like buying a car or taking a trip. For goals like these, funds that "buy and hold" instead of "buy and sell" have an important tax advantage.

If a fund buys and sells all the time, it causes problems. The tax problem is that when a fund sells a stock for more than it paid for it, the fund incurs a capital gain. That capital gain becomes taxable to you as a shareowner in the mutual fund. If the fund had just held on to that higher-priced stock, then you wouldn't owe a tax on the capital gain until you took your money from the fund.

Why do actively managed funds buy and sell so often? It's because they're trying to beat the market. When they correctly predict that a stock will go up and make their gain from holding it, they want to sell and lock in that gain in case the stock later falls.

Index funds don't do much buying and selling. They're not switching in and out of stocks to make a gain. They buy and sell just to match the flows of money coming in and out from investors. This generates only a tiny amount of capital gains, and so you typically owe only a small amount of tax from these operations.

Another Important Leakage: Costs

Taxes are an important leakage from your investments, but not the only one. For some kinds of investments, the costs of getting and holding the investment are considerable.

The good news is that mutual funds have to disclose all these costs. They'll be in a prospectus, the formal document outlining terms and conditions of buying and holding an investment. Costs always include the expenses of administering the fund, doing such things as answering the phone and taking care of customers.

The bad news is that many people don't read or understand the prospectus. As a result, people invest money every day in mutual funds with horrendous costs. In addition to the costs inherent in any mutual fund, costs may also include:

☐ front-end charges, which you must pay just to get into the fund
☐ back-end charges or "redemption fees," which you must pay to get money back out
☐ fees known as "12(b)1" fees, which are charged to all shareholders in some funds to cover distribution-related expenses.

There's no need to pay these fees if you don't have to, and a number of funds are available that don't charge these extra fees. Appendix one of this book lists the specific funds that I recommend for avoiding these fees, together with contact information on the funds.

The numbers on costs are similar to the numbers on taxes earlier in this chapter. If you could make a million dollars over the years by investing in a low-cost fund, that amount could drop to less than half if you invested in a high-cost fund.

The effects of high costs are especially dramatic with some insurance products that are aggressively marketed over the phone. High commissions, right up front, keep the value of your investment from growing much at all in the early years of the insurance plan. You put in hundreds or thousands of dollars, but the cash value of your holding is minimal because most of that is paying the sales commissions. Things get better in the later years of these plans, of course. Still, you can save yourself from these bad deals by resolving not to buy anything over the phone from someone who found you.

A Different Kind of Leakage

Costs and taxes are leakages in that they cause money to leak out of your investment account. I'd like to close this chapter by addressing a different kind of leakage. This is when the money doesn't leak out of the account at all, but the money in your account goes to uses that you don't approve. There are many ways this could happen:

☐ You might disapprove of tobacco. If you hold broad-based mutual funds, they're almost sure to include some tobacco stock.

☐ You might disapprove of companies that hurt the environment. Broad-based mutual funds will surely include stocks of companies that cause environmental harm.

☐ You might not like the way some companies treat their workers, perhaps discriminating against some workers at home or using cheap labor in overseas sweatshops. With a large sample of companies in a stock fund, you're sure to own some of those stocks too.

☐ You might disapprove of the activities of arms manufacturers, perhaps for their activities making guns or, on the national level, making military supplies and weapons systems. It's hard to avoid owning some of these stocks if you have mutual funds.

There are no easy answers to these concerns, but there are some alternatives.

Hold individual stocks. One possibility is to give up mutual funds and hold individual stocks. You would own only the stocks of companies you had checked out. This would be time-consuming and expensive. It would also require you to give up the advantages of diversification and low costs that come with mutual funds.

Buy "socially responsible" mutual funds. Some mutual funds pledge to buy only the stocks of socially responsible companies. Although they can't achieve the diversification, returns and low costs of other mutual funds, they can stick to their definitions of "socially responsible." Unfortunately, their definitions might not match yours, in which case you would still be supporting some socially irresponsible companies—or unnecessarily forgoing ownership of companies that you'd consider socially responsible.

Rationalize holding index funds. When you hold an index fund that seeks to duplicate the performance of the total stock market, you own only tiny representative bits of each company. You could consider yourself as making the statement "I'm supplying investment funds to the economy at large. I don't approve or disapprove of what these companies do." Then you could resolve that with the money you earned, you would do only things that met your definition of social responsibility.

Don't hold stocks. In the next chapter we'll have a look at bonds, an alternative investment to stocks. When you own stock, as we saw, you own a piece of a company—but when you own bonds, you're only a lender. This is a very small difference, morally. If you're a critic of tobacco companies, would you feel more comfortable implicitly lending money to a tobacco company than owning a piece of it?

However you decide this issue, make sure you understand one thing: no matter what you do, your money supports things you don't like. Whenever you buy an investment, your money goes to someone else, who may then do something you don't approve. This is true even when you buy an ordinary good or service. That money is paying someone, who may then go out and do something with the money you don't approve.

I once worked with an organization that wanted to invest its money in a socially responsible way. It had rather tight criteria, wanting to avoid investments in alcohol, tobacco and arms makers. These were criteria I very much respected, and after some consultations, I helped the organization purchase shares in a fund that invested in U.S. government securities. The group was satisfied, but I had a nagging doubt. The U.S. government did many things that the same organization disapproved of, such as U.S. military operations.

Although this book is not an income tax guide, taxes do affect an important issue for many Christians: the peace issue. The traditional peace churches (Mennonite, Brethren, Amish and Friends, for example) do not support war and do not support most of the expenditures we label as "defense." (Billions of that expenditure is decidedly not defensive but offensive in nature.)

The peace issue is only part of the story. Governments do many things that individual Christians may oppose as a matter of conscience, from funding abortions to carrying out capital punishment. How, then, can people of conscience protest the use of their tax money for something they abhor?

Civil disobedience is one possibility, simply refusing to pay taxes and going to jail to avoid supporting an abhorrent practice. Another possibility is "constructive redirection." Here's how it works: Pay the absolute minimum tax that you can, using every legal means to avoid paying more. Then use the money you saved to fund something you do support. If you're currently careless with your taxes and pay $1,000 too much, then by being careful you can save that money next year and give it to a local food bank or homeless ministry.

Jesus was once asked if people should pay taxes to the government of the time, headed by the Roman Caesar. "Then Jesus said to them, 'Give to Caesar what is Caesar's and to God what is God's' " (Mark 12:17). He didn't tell them to give more to Caesar than what was due—but he didn't encourage them to cheat on their taxes either.

Taxes, costs and other leakages can have a profound effect on your investments. You can lose important amounts of money if you ignore them.

Group Study Activities and Questions

1. On a piece of paper, complete this sentence: "What I dislike the most about taxes is _____." Pass in your paper to the group leader, who will read aloud all responses from the study group members.

a. Do all the reasons for disliking taxes really come down to having to give up money?

b. Do you dislike the sales tax, which is automatically tacked on to purchases at the cash register in most jurisdictions?

c. Do you believe that the income tax, as currently administered, is fair?

d. Do you believe that injustices in the current tax system justify the underreporting of income, to avoid giving money to a corrupt system?

2. Is it possible to save large amounts of money for retirement but still "live for today"? Or does saving for retirement necessarily make you more forward-looking and more worried?

3. Suppose a worker buys some shares of her company's stock through an employee stock purchase plan, and suppose that after a time the worker is free to do whatever she wants with the stock. Is it disloyal for her to sell it and put the proceeds into a mutual fund?

4. Would you invest in a pornography company's stock to get high returns? How about a tobacco company or a company that sells alcoholic beverages? How about a mortgage bank that lends money to people whose lifestyles you don't approve of? Or to put it another way, how can you invest money and be sure that you won't be supporting something you disapprove of?

5. Many investors prefer not to invest, directly or indirectly, in the stocks of companies that produce tobacco, because of tobacco's role in causing illness. Should they also withhold their investment funds from restaurant chains that serve large amounts of high-fat foods, also implicated in causing illness? Why or why not?

6. Read Mark 12:13-17.

a. Why were the Pharisees and Herodians asking Jesus about taxes? Was it that they wanted to be sure to live a faithful life?

b. In verse 17, what is Caesar's? Today, what do we owe to the government?

c. In verse 17, what is God's? What do we owe to God?

8

Bonds & Bond Funds

Don't put all your eggs in one basket.
ANONYMOUS

IF YOU RUN TO GRANDMA'S HOUSE with all the eggs in a single basket, you could break them all if you fall down. That's the quaint origin of the saying. It's also part of the rationale behind index fund investing in stocks. You buy a little bit of hundreds or thousands of stocks, and therefore you don't lose much if any one of your stocks does poorly.

Now it's time to see that there are other baskets out there, beyond stocks. For instance, there are separate assets called bonds. Unlike stocks, they don't make you part owner of a company. Instead they amount to promises to repay. When you buy a $1,000 government bond, for instance, you give up your money in return for the government's promise to pay back the $1,000 in a specified way with interest.

With stocks, the amount of money you get paid in any given quarter or year depends on what the company's board of directors decides. It's always possible for a board to decide, "Hey, we didn't make much money and we need to keep all this profit for internal expansion." In that case the board might suspend the dividend and you wouldn't get anything. Also, if a company goes bankrupt, the shareholders are just about last in line to get any of the remaining assets. Other creditors get most of what's there.

All this makes it risky, in general, to hold stocks. Bonds are sold with more guarantees and are in some ways safer.

How Bond Investing Works

When you invest in bonds, you're loaning out your money. The bond is what you get in return, and it states what payments you'll receive in return for that loan.

On a bond, the company pledges to pay interest and principal on time. It's not like a stock, which will pay no dividend at all from time to time if that's what the board of directors decides. Although it's possible that a company will default on a bond and not pay back on time or at all, that's not something a company would do casually.

If you were holding a good-quality bond that was worth $10,000 as its face value and paid 6 percent interest, then each year you would get a total of $600 in interest. If the company didn't make much money, you would still get the $600, almost certainly. Therefore a bond should hold its value relatively well when stocks aren't holding their value.

This greater safety comes at a cost. Specifically, safer bonds don't provide as great a long-term return as do stocks. That's only natural. If bonds, being safer, provided as much return as riskier stocks, then who would want the stocks? When risks and returns have settled out, getting a higher return means you face more risk. This suggests, at the very least, that when someone is offering you a higher return, you should ask about the risk. It's bound to be greater.

Differences Among Bonds

The differences among the bonds you could buy are great. All of the differences relate, in one way or another, to the risk you face when investing in them.

The issuer. Some bonds are issued by small start-up companies. If you buy these bonds, you might lose all your money. Other bonds are issued by the U.S. government, and they are so safe that they're sometimes called a "riskless" asset. They're not totally riskless, but they're about as close as you can get.

The backing. Different security is offered for different kinds of bonds. Mortgage bonds are backed by property, and the bondholders can claim it to get their money back if there is a default. So-called junk bonds aren't backed by property and so are riskier. They pay higher returns in compensation for the risk.

The interest rate. Those who issue bonds have to pay competitive interest rates to get their bonds accepted. What's "competitive" differs from time to time, though. The face-value interest rates on bonds will be different, depending on when they were issued. When interest rates go up, newly issued bonds pay more. This makes existing bonds worth less than before, since their face-value interest isn't as high.

Time to payoff. When a bond reaches maturity, the bondholder gets the original amount back. That's in addition to the interest payments received in the meantime. If a bond from a sound company is just about to mature, say, in the next month, then there's very little risk in holding it. If a bond doesn't mature for thirty more years, then there's a lot of risk. Lots of things could happen in thirty years, not all of them good.

Because of all these factors, there are thousands of different kinds of bonds you could hold, each with its own characteristics. How does an individual investor decide which ones to buy? On a more practical level, since $10,000 is a small bond in the bond market, and since most people don't have $10,000 to invest, how are bonds a practical investment at all?

The answer is to give up trying to pick bonds and avoid holding bonds directly. That is, you buy mutual funds that invest in the total bond market. Like stock mutual funds, they pool the money of thousands of investors and buy bonds in large quantities. They collect interest on the bonds, collect and reinvest principal as bonds mature, and pass through the earnings to those who have invested.

If you invest in the entire bond market through a bond mutual fund, it doesn't matter whether corporate bonds or government bonds are a better deal. You own both. It doesn't matter whether short-maturity or long-maturity bonds are a better deal. You own both. It doesn't even matter much whether a particular issuer defaults on its bonds, since any one issue is a tiny part of your holdings. Just as with stock funds, you avoid risking your money on whether any one company or sector is better than another. You get approximately the return on the whole bond market.

As with stock funds, there are actively managed bond funds. Their managers try to beat the market by predicting which kinds of bonds will do better than others and then buying more of those. As hard as it is to beat the stock market, it may be even harder to beat the bond market, and so actively managed bond funds often do no better than the market. The one thing that doesn't change is that paying analysts and managers to try to beat the market costs money. After expenses are considered, most actively managed bond funds do worse than funds that avoid active management.

The bottom line is that the best way to make money over the long term in the bond market is to buy and hold index funds. Sounds familiar, doesn't it? With bond index funds you get the average return to the bond market, but with below-average costs, because the fund isn't paying managers and analysts in a (frequently futile) effort to beat the market.

Christians thinking of investing in bond funds or even money market funds must think carefully about biblical prohibitions on receiving interest. No matter how good an investment is, we don't want to hold it if it's wrong, biblically speaking.

At first the Old Testament appears to contain a fairly broad prohibition on lending money for interest. Deuteronomy 23:19 says, "Do not charge your brother interest, whether on money or food or anything else that may earn interest." However, the next verse continues: "You may charge a foreigner interest, but not a brother Israelite, so that the LORD your God may bless you in everything you put your hand to in the land you are entering to possess" (Deuteronomy 23:20).

The prohibition against charging interest, then, seems to have applied among the children of Israel but not in arm's-length transactions with foreigners. When, as today, corporations are owned by people of all faiths and serve customers of all faiths, the transactions can only be regarded as arm's length.

Still, it is clear in the New Testament that believers are sometimes called to make loans without interest—or even the return of principal! Luke 6:34-35 says:

> If you lend to those from whom you expect repayment, what credit is that to you? Even "sinners" lend to "sinners," expecting to be repaid in full. But love your enemies, do good to them, and lend to them without expecting to get anything back. Then your reward will be great, and you will be sons of the Most High, because he is kind to the ungrateful and wicked.

If we are to grow spiritually, we are called—at least some of the time—to lend without expecting repayment.

Remember that bonds usually have a lower return and less risk than stocks. That makes the higher costs of actively managed bond funds especially troublesome. When a high-flying, high-performing stock fund loses a couple of percentage points to higher costs, the shareholders might not notice. Those same costs would be a much higher proportion of the modest return of a bond fund. Those costs would eat up a large part of the gain to be had over the years.

If you're a small investor and don't have enough money to hold both a stock index fund and a bond index fund, there are balanced funds for you. They hold a blend of stocks and bonds in the same fund. By holding a single fund, you can get the high average returns of stocks and the risk reduction that comes from having part of your holdings in bonds. A top-notch balanced fund is recommended in appendix one, at the back of this book.

How Much to Hold in Bonds?

We started this chapter with the proverb "Don't put all your eggs in one basket." Following that advice, we shouldn't invest all our money in a small number of stocks, or certainly in one stock. Diversifying by investing in a broad-based index fund is usually better. But we don't have to stop there, now that there are bond index funds. Now it's easy to put our eggs into thousands of different "baskets"—thousands of stocks and bonds.

Stocks will have a higher return over time, if the past is any guide. They'll also have a higher risk. If you invested $10,000 in stock funds and held them thirty years, then with long-term average returns your money would grow to $228,923. But you'd also face the possibility of a loss as bad as 43 percent in any one year. (That's the worst year from 1926 to 2001.) It would take discipline and maturity to avoid panicking with that kind of a loss.

Now hold half your money in bonds and see what happens. If you invested $10,000 in a 50-50 combination of stock and bond funds, with long-term average returns your money would grow to $125,564. That's a lot less than the $228,923 you'd get with all stock—but then your worst yearly loss would be only around 22 percent.

Want still more safety? Then you can hold a money market fund, where your $10,000, growing at 4.5 percent, would reach only $37,453. You would not find your money worth less at the end of a year—but see how little it would grow? If you can stand to see your investments go up and down without panicking, you can do much better over the long run than with "safe" investments.

All this means that the allocation of our assets between stocks and bonds will depend partly on our risk preferences and partly on our situation in life.

A young person saving for retirement forty years away can afford to go entirely into stocks, since the ups and downs should average out over time to yield the traditionally higher returns of stocks. Someone already retired should have much less stock, proportionately. The stock market has been depressed at times for years on end. This can mean a hardship for that retired person, who may have to sell off stocks at bargain-basement prices to get income for living expenses.

What Is Market Timing?

There are considerable advantages to having large holdings of bonds when stocks are not doing well. The bonds will hold their value better and pay a more reliable return. That leads some people to wonder about a strategy of "market timing": shifting money into stocks when the stock market is about to go up, then pulling money out before the stock market goes down.

I need to be clear about this: consistently successful market timing is impossible. Don't try it.

Many individual investors have been badly hurt by trying to time the market. Here's why: The best time to shift money into stocks is when they're low-priced. When they're low-priced, however, it's typically a time of pessimism, when people think stocks are not going to do very well. To buy stocks at such a time takes more nerve than most individual investors can summon up.

On the other hand, the best time to shift money out of stocks is when they're high-priced. That's usually a time of great optimism, when people believe stocks could only go higher and higher.

You have to make two very difficult decisions to correctly time the market. You have to get out at the right time, when stocks have gotten very high—and then you also have to get back in. I know someone who successfully took tens of thousands of dollars out of the stock market in a retirement fund shortly before a 20 percent drop in the market. But then he didn't know when to get back in. The market went up another 20 percent and more, and he still didn't get back in.

Even among market pros, market timing is considered poison. Market timing is an especially destructive departure from "buy and hold." Remember that the best long-term strategy is to buy and hold.

Rules, I Want Rules

General discussions don't solve the problem of how much money you should put into stocks and bonds. I'll show you some pretty good rules now, but even when you follow a sensible rule, regrets are possible. After the fact, we'll know whether stocks outperformed bonds in any given period. With perfect hindsight, we'll know that we could have allocated 100 percent to stocks or 100 percent to bonds—and have made more money than we did. Because our foresight is imperfect, 100 percent in either direction is not a good choice. Here are the rules:

☐ *60 percent stocks, 40 percent bonds.* This is a pretty good rule. If you read no further and put 60 percent of your money into stocks and 40 percent into bonds, you won't go far wrong. In fact, this is such a good overall percentage that one of the best mutual funds has that percentage written into its structure. It always holds 60 percent stocks, 40 percent bonds, no matter what its managers think will happen to stocks and bonds in the future. For most people, 60-40 should be far better than having 100 percent of your holdings in either stocks or bonds.

☐ *The age-percent rule.* An old rule of thumb advises you to write down your age—say, thirty-five. The rule says then to put a percentage sign behind that number and put that part of your holdings into bonds. The thirty-five-year-old would put 35 percent into bonds. Finally, the rule of thumb says, put the rest into stocks—65 percent in this case. As your age increases over time, you gradually put more into bonds and less, proportionately, into stocks. If you live to be one hundred while following this rule, by then you're entirely into bonds. The good thing about the age-percent rule is that it has you automatically investing a lot in stocks early in life and more in bonds later on. That's a sensible pattern, because you want the higher return of stocks if you're just starting out and the reduced risk of bonds if you're retired. The bad thing about the rule is that it may underweight stocks. Many advisers believe a twenty-five-year-old should be entirely in stocks, not 75 percent in stocks, as the rule would indicate. Also, many advisers think that even a one hundred-year-old should have some money in stocks. The age-percent rule is a good, but decidedly not perfect, rule.

☐ *Following a broker's asset allocation advice.* Some brokerages issue asset allocation advice. They make recommendations about how much of your holdings should be in stocks and bonds—and cash, for that matter. They change these recommendations based on how they think stocks are going to do. Oddly enough, it's not at all certain that you'll do better following a broker's asset allocation advice. *The Wall Street Journal* runs a little asset allocation contest of sorts. It asks major brokerages for their advice, then checks how those allocations would do against something it calls a "robot blend"—a fixed allocation between stocks and bonds. The robot blend frequently outperforms some brokers' recommendations.

For the Extremely Cautious

Sometimes people are so cautious that they want to avoid stocks altogether. Often these people are older and can remember times when stocks lost huge amounts of value and banks failed. I sympathize with these feelings, but they can lead to bad investment decisions.

The reason is that there are many risks to guard against. Focusing on any one risk to the exclusion of others is a mistake. If you hold 100 percent bonds, you don't face the risk of the stock market, but you do face the risk that some bond issuers would default. You also face a risk that a future inflation of prices would leave your income insufficient to cover living expenses. It is actually less risky to hold a blend of stocks and bonds than to hold 100 percent bonds.

The following technique may work with some extra-cautious people. I'll show you a way to guarantee, with U.S. government backing, that you will not lose a penny—although you may make a great deal of money in the stock market. Take half of your investment money and put it into U.S. government securities. By choosing the securities and calculating their doubling time correctly, you can be guaranteed that this 50 percent of your money will grow back to the original sum. At current interest rates, for example, think about what would happen to $10,000. Half of that, or $5,000, can be guaranteed to grow back to the original $10,000 in thirteen years. Then take the other 50 percent and invest it in a stock market index fund. Even if the stock market becomes totally worthless over that time, you'll have your original $10,000. If the stock market has anything other than total catastrophe, you'll get back a good deal more than your original $10,000.

That's not to say a 50-50 allocation is necessarily good—only to show that you can control risk, even while you get some money to work harder for you in the stock market

Christians naturally look forward to the time prophesied in the Bible when we will live on a perfect earth. We wonder, too, about prophesied times of suffering and tribulation and their relationship to the return of Christ.

This has a direct impact on our financial lives if we believe that a time of testing, of biblical proportions, is drawing near. There have been cases in which people sold all their goods and went to mountaintops to await the end.

Unfortunately, even some otherwise levelheaded Christian writers have encouraged people to take extreme action because an economic cataclysm was coming. While it's always sensible to be prepared, it's also important to understand what our role should be in a time of great testing. We should be there in the thick of it to serve our fellow men and women, not holed up in a mountain retreat with food and guns to shoot our hungry and desperate neighbors.

If I believed Christ was coming tomorrow to end this phase of human history, what would be my recommended allocation of stocks and bonds? It wouldn't matter! The size of our portfolios won't make the slightest difference when Christ returns.

Group Study Activities and Questions

1. On a piece of paper, complete this sentence: "If I thought that Jesus Christ would be returning to earth tomorrow, then tonight I would _____." Pass the results to the group leader, who will record the responses on a flip chart or chalkboard.

a. What is the most prevalent answer among the members of your group?

b. Can you do enough good works in a day to assure your salvation? In a week? In a year? In a lifetime?

c. How much of your preparation for Christ's coming would be financial?

2. Complete the sentence "If I thought the world and national economies were going to collapse in six months, before that happened I would _____." Pass the results to the group leader.

a. How much effort would you devote toward getting food—and the guns to defend it with?

b. Do you think you would be prepared at the end of the six months?

c. Would you take money, with penalties, out of your retirement fund to prepare for the collapse?

d. Would you be more confident in making radical financial changes if Christian leaders and authors began warning that an "economic earthquake" was coming?

3. Suppose a stranger came to your town claiming that he had invented "the next Frisbee," a plastic toy that would become as successful as the original Frisbee. He wants you to lend him $1,000 for a year while he begins manufacturing and selling this toy. What rate of interest would he have to promise to get you to lend him your money? What does your answer say about risk and return?

4. What if a financial planner told you, "Everyone needs to have some underperforming assets, whether it's bonds, stocks or whatever. If all of your assets have done well, that's a sign you haven't diversified enough—and you won't have any money in 'losers' that are about to become winners." Would you agree? Would you want to have some underperforming assets among your investments? Would you trust this financial planner more or less than a planner who said you should never keep underperforming assets?

5. Why do investment professionals say that you have to make two correct decisions in order to "time the market"? How much effort should you spend monitoring the stock market and shifting between stocks and bonds?

6. Read Luke 6:30-38. Is Jesus giving financial advice in these verses? Do you believe that this passage forbids Christians from investing in bond funds that seek to pay back investors' principal plus interest?

9

Avoiding Investment Mistakes

If it sounds too good to be true, it usually is.
ANONYMOUS

THE INVESTMENT APPROACH outlined so far in this book has a lot to recommend it. In recent decades, buying and holding index funds has been a superior way for an unsophisticated investor to make an investment grow. The strategy is simple and straightforward. Further, it avoids the problems that come from worrying about how to make a higher return than everybody else. It settles for getting the average return that everybody else is making. After all, that's what a broad-based market index is—an average of what everybody else is making. Of course, this strategy doesn't involve the expense of trying to beat the return everyone else is making. "Admitting defeat" turns into "declaring victory" when you achieve the average return with below-average expenses, allowing you to keep more of that average return to meet your financial goals.

The biggest single problem, I have discovered, is getting people to adopt this powerful strategy. Here's why: Very few people out there have a financial interest in getting investors into low-cost, efficient index funds. On the other hand, many people have a financial interest in getting investors to do something else. In this chapter we'll see some of the mistakes that investors can make. Most of the mistakes stem from wanting to get more, in a financial setting that's not very favorable to small investors who want to beat the market return.

Mistake 1: Buying Any Investment That's Pushed over the Phone

If someone calls you to push an investment, say no. The best investments—low-cost, efficient funds—aren't aggressively marketed. If you want to buy good investments, you have to seek them out. On the other hand, the investments that are aggressively marketed usually are a bad deal. They often involve heavy costs and loads, including the costs of the telemarketing that pushes the investments on you in the first place.

Mistake 2: Buying Any Investment Under Time Pressure

Stock and bond index funds are available every business day of the year. If you don't buy today, they'll be there tomorrow on much the same terms. Of course, the market may go up today, making them more expensive, or go down today, making them cheaper. But there won't be any particular reason to buy on any given day.

Therefore, if someone calls and tells you that a particular investment will be available "only until Monday," that's a bad sign. The best investments are available every business day.

Another good test of an investment is to tell the person selling the investment, "I want to look at your printed material and think some more before investing." Any ethical seller of investments will respond by saying something like "Take your time, and let me know if you have any questions." There will be no sales pressure.

If you sense sales pressure or a reluctance to send printed material, drop that investment as fast as you can.

I have a Christian friend who asked me to check out an investment he was considering. He had received a telemarketing call. Ordinarily he wouldn't have considered the investment, but the caller identified himself as someone who had formerly been associated with a respected evangelist.

The caller applied increasing sales pressure, calling back several times and telling him he'd have to invest "by Monday" if he wanted to get in. The caller also was reluctant to send the full details of the investment in print form.

The investment, it turned out, was a dubious insurance product with huge sales loads and no merit for my friend. It was being sold in high-pressure fashion by someone trying to exploit my friend's trust that a fellow Christian would not take advantage of him.

This is not a new problem. In the time of Peter's ministry there were false teachers who exploited the trust of fellow believers (2 Peter 2:3). Modern technology, however, has made it possible to abuse trust on a large scale.

Mistake 3: Abandoning Index Funds Too Soon

The first two mistakes—buying pushed investments and buying under time pressure—are easy to recognize. Other mistakes are more subtle. Going to actively managed funds instead of index funds too soon is one, though this decision can be made to sound quite reasonable.

One fact you need to know is this: it's not easy to do better than buying and holding index funds. With this strategy you won't greatly underperform the market and your money will grow nicely over the long term. But if you become a much more sophisticated investor over time, you may become restless with buying and holding index funds. At that point you may actually be ready to leave index funds behind. It's a problem, however, when some financial advisers push you to abandon index funds when you know that you're still a financial novice. What arguments will they make?

Some financial advisers will tell you that when you buy an index fund you are "settling for mediocrity." In a sense, you are. You won't beat the market averages; you will (roughly) match the market averages if you hold index funds. You will experience lower costs and taxes, however, so you'll be better off than the average investor.

Often the financial advisers that pooh-pooh index funds are offering actively managed funds. These funds go to the expense of hiring managers and analysts in an effort to beat the market. In turn, they charge you those expenses—and often many other expenses and loads as well. They not only have to beat the market; they also have to beat it by a substantial margin to leave you better off than if you had invested in index funds. More than half the time, they fail.

It's important to read the fine print when someone's talking you out of buying and holding low-cost index funds. You will be told that a fund you're being offered has beaten the performance of index funds in the past. The fine print will often say something like "Past performance does not guarantee future results." Well, believe it! They have to include that disclosure legally, and it is true.

When a mutual fund company offers lots of funds, certainly some of them in a given period will beat the returns to holding index funds. But can they keep it up? Probably not.

Imagine how some totally truthful advertising would make those funds look. "We'll use your money to try to beat the market averages. We'll spend a lot of your money, both in trying to pick stocks that will outperform the market and in getting new shareholders in. More than half the time, we'll probably fail. But we'll heavily promote the small proportion of cases in which we do outperform the market, even though we can't guarantee that such performance will continue. The one thing you can count on is that we'll spend more of your money running our fund than would a low-cost index fund."

I have a little two-way test for when you think you have learned enough that you can beat the strategy of buying and holding index funds. When (1) your holdings are more than $500,000 and (2) you understand every financial term in Burton Malkiel's book *A Random Walk down Wall Street,* you're ready. Keep in mind that $500,000 doesn't make you a big player in asset markets. Keep in mind also that understanding *A Random Walk down Wall Street* doesn't mean you're a financial expert. (It's not an investments textbook or research volume.) But if you don't meet my two-way test, you have little hope of swimming with the big fish in the asset markets. You'll only beat the market averages by blind luck.

If you *do* meet the two-way test, you'll know how difficult it is to do better than buying and holding index funds. Then, if you prefer, buy actively managed funds. Don't do it sooner. And consider this: the investment company TIAA-CREF—one of the world's largest retirement systems, with some of the brightest analysts around— runs its actively managed funds with a combination of stock picking and indexing, not stock picking alone. Further, right now TIAA-CREF's highest-performing retirement fund is its own stock index fund, not any of its funds that use active management!

Mistake 4: Buying Individual Stocks
Using the "Story" Approach

There's a lot of appeal to buying individual stocks. You can imagine that you're a great tycoon or financier as you put some of your saved money into the stock of a particular company. You can imagine that you, through your cleverness, have come up with a way to multiply your money. Or you may just like a certain company because it has local plants or outlets.

You won't, on average, beat the market by buying individual stocks. Think about it like this: A total stock market index fund approximates the return to the overall stock market. Meanwhile, some investors in individual stocks are doing better than the average, some are doing worse and others are matching the average. All together, they are achieving the market average. That's the definition of the average.

While all those investors are achieving the market average, however, they're doing it at higher costs. They're paying fees for buying and selling stocks, and they're doing it with much less convenience than a good mutual fund will offer. On average, they're getting average returns—but at above-average costs.

People love to think they can make money with the "story approach" to stocks. They think up a story, often well based in reality, then invest accordingly. For example, someone looks at the population, sees a large number of middle-aged people and concludes, "These people will need nursing home care when they get older. Nursing homes will make a lot of money. I'll invest in nursing home stocks and get rich!"

Why won't this work? Because other people already have recognized these well-known population trends and bought stock based on them. Investors now will make money on this "story" only if nursing homes make more money *than was expected.* The addition to nursing home revenue from an aging population was already expected. The real question is whether the additions will be greater than expected—and on this, the individual investor typically has no advantage in judging.

Here's a common story: Someone realizes that in the fourth quarter of each year sales of toys boom. The conclusion? "I'll buy toy company stocks in September, then the company will make a lot of money in October, November and December. When all that money rolls in, the stock will go up and I'll sell in December. I'll get rich!"

Why won't this work? Because other people have already recognized that fourth-quarter sales of toys are high. Investors will make money on this "story" only if toy companies make more money *than was expected.* And how can an individual investor know whether this year's toy sales forecasts for the fourth quarter are too low?

The plain fact is that to make money on "stories," you have to get the story right—and you have to come up with the story first. Or you have to know whether others in the stock market are underestimating the impact of the story. Neither is likely.

People often try out stories with investment professionals. You can see a lot of the story approach if you watch *Wall Street Week* on Public TV, especially the section that answers readers' letters. A reader will write that he's observed people are spending more money in drive-through lines at fast food places. How can he make money on this observation in the stock market?

Watch the facial expressions of the guest panelists carefully when they answer a question like this. You'll see that they know they're taking part in a big joke when they answer. Why? Because here, as with so many "stories," there's money to be made only if others haven't already capitalized on the story. A guest panelist's answer to a question like this would probably touch on the leading companies in the fast food industry—but would not include a direct answer to the question "How can I make money on this fact in the stock market?" The expert generally won't state the most important fact: you can't make money on this observation on drive-throughs unless the rest of the market is not sufficiently aware of this fact.

Finally, what if you absolutely *have* to put some money into individual stocks? If you can't resist the urge, then make it a small amount. Allocate a small percentage of your holdings to individual stocks. Don't be tempted to risk more. Go ahead and play "stories" or hot tips from the hairdresser or whatever. All the while, keep in mind that the probabilities are against you. On average, you won't do better than an index fund. When you do better than average, it will most often be pure luck and not the "story" that you have played.

Mistake 5: Confusing a Booming Market with Genius

Mistake five is just an extension of mistake four, investing in individual stocks using the "story" approach, but it's a real problem when the stock market overall is going up. In such times it's possible for people to be following a losing strategy and not know it.

When the market is booming, stocks are generally higher today than yesterday. That means that, on average, even a totally bogus "story" about a stock will result in gains. Suppose you think Coca-Cola stock will go up because there will be an invasion from Mars (and the Martians like Coke, and they always politely pay for soft drinks, even though they're invaders). This bogus "story" will usually result in gains for the investor who buys Coca-Cola stock during a booming market. Only a few stocks go down in a booming market, after all.

If it's possible to make money with a story about the Martians, then it's surely possible to make money with equally crazy but more respectable-sounding economic "theories." People will advance theories about technology generating never-ending profits, about our economy having solved the problem of scarcity—the story doesn't matter if the market is up overall. Any theory predicting higher stock prices will be embraced, and most any strategy of buying stocks will work. Some lucky people will beat the market averages and will think they have learned to beat the market consistently.

For all these reasons, in a booming market there will be people playing pet theories on individual stocks and thinking they're geniuses. They'll be wrong—but will they be worse off than index investors? Yes, for two reasons. First, they'll be buying and selling at higher costs than are available through index funds. Second, they'll be subject to the risks inherent in owning a single stock. A strike against that company or an unfavorable regulatory ruling or a disastrous product recall will drag the company's stock down.

This is a place where envy can be a real problem. People will hear neighbors talking about the killing they have made in stocks and become less satisfied with the plodding returns of index funds. They should understand that individual investors, as a group, don't consistently beat the market. Some may talk about the money they have made but fail to compare it with how much the market overall went up. Many people who *think* they have beaten the market have not.

There is also a part of human nature involved here. If your neighbor made two investments, one for no gain and one for a 40 percent return, which one do you think you'll hear about? Don't be discouraged if your index fund strategy returned "only" 20 percent over that same time period. That return may be the same as your neighbor's overall return—or even higher, when you factor in the part that your neighbor didn't talk about.

Mistake 6: Going for the "Hot Sector"

When you buy and hold broad-based index funds, you are investing in every sector of the economy represented in the stock market. That's fine, but couldn't you increase your return by investing more in the hot sectors and less in the slow sectors of the economy?

You could, but only if you could identify in advance the sectors of the market that will outperform the others. That is quite difficult to do, as it turns out. Around the year 2000, there was a great deal of excitement about technology and communications stocks. Technology and communication were about to change our lives. Surely these stocks would make us rich.

Wrong. It was true that technology and communication companies were poised to make a great deal of money, but this was not a new prediction. The prices of those stocks already reflected the presumed high profits. There would be unusual gains in holding these stocks, not if there were "just" great gains, but only if the gains were greater than expected. In many cases the gains were less than expected, as hoped-for profits failed to materialize.

The best investment strategy for a small investor, then, was not to bet on high-tech companies (concentrating an investment in that sector). Nor was the best strategy to bet against the high-tech companies by withdrawing from that sector. The best strategy was to invest in high-tech companies only to the extent they were represented in index funds.

As time goes by, there will be other "hot sectors." Fortunes will be made and lost by people trading in and out of the associated stocks. Meanwhile, those holding index funds will have a smart amount invested in each hot sector—the amount represented by that kind of investment in the overall market index.

 In Ecclesiastes the Teacher wrote the following:

The race is not to the swift
  or the battle to the strong,
nor does food come to the wise
  or wealth to the brilliant
  or favor to the learned;
but time and chance happen to them all. (Ecclesiastes 9:11)

The Teacher was commenting on the unfairness of life. This could equally well apply to financial markets. In investment the race really isn't to the swift, if "the swift" is the one who is chasing the hot sector rather than sticking with a well-diversified investment program.

The Teacher clearly saw the folly of wealth. He had a great deal of wealth himself. Indeed, some scholars identify the Teacher as Solomon, Israel's richest king. Had the wealth brought him happiness? Apparently not. The Teacher wrote:

Whoever loves money never has money enough;
  Whoever loves wealth is never satisfied with his income.
  This too is meaningless. (Ecclesiastes 5:10)

Even wealth of biblical proportions can become routine. A wealthy person can come to regard great wealth as normal—and "meaningless."

Mistake 7: Bailing Out When the Market Goes Down

Financial markets go up and down. Sometimes they go down a lot. When they do, the people who lose the most are the ones who get out then. They sell their assets at prices reflecting all the pessimism that follows a crash in values.

You can get some good laughs from telling people the key to making money in the stock market is to "buy low, sell high." It's so obvious, it's funny. Yet often the small players—the "small fish"—do the opposite and hurt themselves badly in the stock market.

Here's how it happens: When the stock market is high and optimism reigns, small fish get into the market. People can't see how the market could do anything but go up and up. Eventually, however, the market does go down. It's as inevitable as the law of gravity. Now pessimism has taken over and people can't see how the market will go up again. The small fish sell and get out. They have lost money. That is, the small fish have succeeded in buying high and selling low!

Certainly it would increase your wealth to buy when stocks are low and sell out just as the market reaches a top. But that's market timing, and it's close to impossible. If you try to execute a perfect strategy, getting in and out of the market at just the right time, you're likely to lose a lot. Just staying in the market is good, not perfect—but the perfect is the enemy of the good.

The best strategy for avoiding market timing is this: buy the same dollar amount of your funds faithfully every month. This discipline will get you some bargains over the years. When the market has just gone down and people are pessimistic, you'll be buying your usual monthly dollar amount. You'll get a higher than usual number of shares because they're a bargain. For that matter, when the market has just gone up, you'll also be buying your usual monthly dollar amount. You'll be avoiding the temptation to sink a lot of money into the market when prices are high.

Putting the same amount of money into the market every month makes a lot of sense. The only thing that doesn't make sense is the term for this: "dollar-cost averaging." Don't try to make sense of that term, just understand that it means "buying the same dollar amount every month."

A steady investment plan can tame your fear of crashes. Yes, there are years when the market's performance is terrible. People sometimes need to be reminded that stocks don't always go up. In 1931, the market's worst year in history, someone holding 100 percent stocks would have had a 43 percent loss.

A bad year is cushioned considerably for someone holding a mix of stocks and bonds. The worst single-year loss amounted to only a 27 percent loss for the investor holding 60 percent stocks and 40 percent bonds. But when you put your money into the market gradually, you can do even better than that. Then only a little of your money has "bought at the top" and more of it has bought at times that stocks were relatively cheap. The long-run performance of that same 60-40 mix, over a sixty-year period, is more than 9 percent. (At that rate, you double your money every eight years on average—if you stay in.)

When you have gotten your finances in order and saved up an emergency fund, you can afford to leave your money alone when the market plunges. That's what you should do. The historical record shows that the real chumps were the ones who sold out when the market crashed.

Mistake 8: Calling Something an Investment
When It's Not an Investment

When you invest, you give up current income and consumption in the hope of making a future return. We have the general idea that "investment" is a good thing. Unfortunately, there are people who take advantage of our favorable feelings about "investment" to try to sell us things that aren't investments at all.

One good example is time-share resort properties. High-pressure salespeople will try to get you to "invest" in a week at Wonder Lake condominiums. If you want to spend that week every year at Wonder Lake and the price is right, fine—but it's not an investment. If you doubt that, just do a little checking. The newspapers near Wonder Lake will have legal notices of auctions every so often. At those auctions they'll be selling time-shares. The legal language will say something like "1/52 interests in resort property."

The story behind this is that the owner of a particular week at Wonder Lake, facing high fees for continuing to own the property, decided to walk away from the commitment. The property was worth so little, compared with maintenance fees, that it had a minimal resale value. Now that's not an investment. How many times do people walk away from bonds or stocks, so that somebody has to pick up the pieces and have an auction?

It's bad enough when we let others pull language tricks on us to get us to spend money. It's worse yet when we delude ourselves. Don't say you decided to "invest" in a sports car unless it truly is an investment.

Resort properties and sports cars might make sense in your spending plan, if you have the money. They have no place in your investment plan.

One More Mistake for Good Measure: Having More, Wanting More

One underappreciated danger of an investment program is that it will succeed too well. Think about this: What level of financial achievement would make you happy? A million dollars? A paid-for house, a reasonable retirement fund and current income sufficient to live a comfortable life? Whatever it is, it's important not to fall into the trap of having more and yet wanting more.

It seems that, for a lot of people, the more they have, the more they want. No matter how well their investments succeed, they aren't satisfied. Their wants have outstripped even a large increase in their financial resources. This is just another application of the happy-o-stat, that internal feeling that tells us that what we have is normal and deserved. In time, we get accustomed to what we have now, even if it's a lot more than we had before.

Therefore it's important at the outset of an investment program to think seriously about how much is enough. If you find yourself wanting more and spending more just because you have more money, you're starting a race you can't win. We humans are clever at thinking up things we "need" if we have enough money to afford them—things we wouldn't have imagined needing at a lower income level.

So how do we fight this? One method is to write down financial goals and periodically review them. Remind yourself how happy you promised yourself you'd feel if you paid off all your debts, for example. Then when you do pay off all your debts, feel happy! Another method is to set a cap on your wealth, as recommended by Christian financial adviser Howard Dayton.* This cap would be a total of all your assets—stocks, bonds, real estate and the rest. Above that amount, you can give away anything you receive. That may sound like a strong measure, but if it keeps you out of the "having more, wanting more" race, it will be well worthwhile. And you can make some worthy recipients very, very happy.

Avoiding Big, Dumb Mistakes
The key to financial success, for most people, is not subtle. The key is not in flawlessly executing a complex strategy. Rather, it's in avoiding big, dumb mistakes.

You won't lose much money by having a 16 percent credit card

—————————————————————————————

*Howard Dayton, *Your Money Counts* (Wheaton, Ill.: Tyndale House, 1996).

when careful shopping would turn up a 14 percent credit card. You can lose thousands by buying things on a credit card when you don't have the money to cover the bill.

You won't lose much by having your allocation 5 percent wrong—say, 60 percent stocks instead of 65 percent. You can lose a fortune by buying investments from unethical and pushy people over the phone.

Most of the mistakes we've been discussing involve one or both of these two elements: (1) getting greedy and (2) overestimating your own financial knowledge. Don't let these mistakes happen to you.

Group Study Activities and Questions

1. Listen in as two members of your study group read the following dialogue aloud. (Or you could be one of those two members!)

[Phone rings.]

TERRY: Hello.

TELEMARKETER: Hello, Terry Reynolds?

TERRY: Yes, this is Terry.

TELEMARKETER: Terry, my name is Chris DeShazo and I'm with United Equity Investments. We're calling financially aware people like yourself to let them in on an outstanding new investment opportunity. Would you like to earn more on your investment dollars?

TERRY: Well, yes, but I'm not interested.

TELEMARKETER: Your name was recommended to us by your former pastor, Robert Underwood. He and other Christians are especially interested in our investment products because they know our firm was founded by a strong Christian . . .

a. How far do telemarketers usually get with you when you get a call like this?

b. Would it make a difference to you if an investment were recommended by a "Christian" investment company?

c. Would you think less of your former pastor if you believed that he had given your name to a company like United Equity Investments?

d. Could you be certain that your former pastor gave your name out, just because the salesperson says that the pastor did?

2. Most people naturally suspect that an investment isn't a good deal if it's pushed on them with a very short time to decide. Why, then, does pushing investments with time pressure work so well?

3. It is well known that buying and selling stocks in a short time is quite risky. It is also well known that holding stocks over a long time period ("buy and hold") is a profitable strategy. Why, then, is the idea of buying and selling stocks frequently in a short period of time so attractive to people? Is buying and selling stocks in a short period just a form of gambling? Is it more respectable than gambling? More fun?

4. Suppose 100,000 people gather in a stadium for a big experiment. Each takes out a regular coin (not a rigged coin) and flips it. Everyone who flips tails has to leave, but everyone who flips heads gets to flip again. After the first round, about half the people are left (50,000). Then 25,000 people are left, and after that, 12,500. After some more rounds, only a handful remain. Are the remaining people good at coin flipping or just lucky?

Thousands of stock analysts try to pick good stocks. Are the ones who pick high-returning stocks good at it or just lucky? How can you tell?

5. Why do people want to apply the word *investment* to an expenditure that's clearly not an investment, like buying a new sports car?

6. Have someone read Ecclesiastes 9:11. What does this passage say to us today? What does it say about our investments? After its survey of the seeming emptiness of life, what conclusion does Ecclesiastes reach (see 12:13-14)?

10

Saving for Big-Ticket Items

Waiting necessarily commands a price.
GUSTAV CASSEL

WAITING COMMANDS A PRICE? That's right. If you get some money but wait to spend it, then you get paid a price for that waiting. If you put money in the bank, that price is interest. If you invest the money, then the price is less certain, but ultimately it's the return you get on that investment.

When we save for big-ticket items, we're taking advantage of the fact that waiting necessarily commands a price. We're deferring spending or consuming today, in order to get more money to meet a financial goal somewhere down the road.

In this chapter we'll look at what's involved in saving for a big-ticket financial goal.

The Importance of Time Horizon
As we have seen, over the long term the best way to become wealthy

is to buy and hold index funds of stocks and bonds. To do that, you have to get control of your budget so that you spend less than you make, and you need to take care of housing, transportation and insurance matters. You also need to have an emergency fund saved up so that you can leave your long-term investments alone.

But all that, especially buying and holding index funds, is advice for the long term. You may have a goal that's more immediate.

Economists and analysts refer to time horizon, in this context, as the time during which investment funds are committed. If you're twenty-five years old and saving for retirement at sixty-five, your time horizon is forty years.

When you're saving for a goal other than retirement, your time horizon is usually shorter. If you're saving for the college education of a newborn, it's about seventeen years. If you're saving to purchase a house, it's however many years until you think you'll be buying.

You can afford to take some risk with long-term funds. Index funds of stocks, following the stock market itself, tend to do well over the years, even as they go up and down sharply in any given year. "Risk" in this setting means having to sell your holdings when they happen to be down.

In fact, it's risky to do anything other than hold substantial amounts of stock if you want long-term growth. The historical averages indicate that holding anything else, including bonds and especially bank deposits, will leave you less well off than if you hold stocks.

Proper investing for retirement, then, should depend heavily on index funds of stocks. Investing for a goal ten years away should likewise depend heavily on stock index funds. When a goal is only five years away, however, it's time to start moving that money out of stocks and into more stable assets, such as bond funds and money market funds. When a goal is only a year away, that money should be safely put away into money market funds—the "super checking accounts" of the financial world.

Some people have been disappointed by trying to leave money in the stock market as long as possible, to earn those high returns. Stocks earn high returns over the long run, but they may lose a substantial part of their value in short-term financial storms.

The lesson is to match the way you save to your time horizon—heavily toward stocks for long-term investments, heavily toward money market funds for anything with a short time horizon.

> Time horizon is important, but it's even more important for Christians to realize that we can't perfectly plot out the future. The future is in God's hands, and we don't know what he has intended for us. As a psalmist wrote:
>
> Show me, O LORD, my life's end
>   and the number of my days;
>   let me know how fleeting is my life.
> You have made my days a mere handbreadth;
>   the span of my years is as nothing before you.
>   Each man's life is but a breath.
> Man is a mere phantom as he goes to and fro:
>   He bustles about, but only in vain;
>   he heaps up wealth, not knowing who will get it.
> But now, Lord, what do I look for?
>   My hope is in you. (Psalm 39:4-7)
>
> Excessive worry about the future is out of place for the Christian. As Jesus taught:
>
> Do not worry, saying, "What shall we eat?" or "What shall we drink?" or "What shall we wear?" For the pagans run after all these things, and your heavenly Father knows that you need them. But seek first his kingdom and his righteousness, and all these things will be given to you as well. Therefore do not worry about tomorrow, for tomorrow will worry about itself. Each day has enough trouble of its own. (Matthew 6:31-34)

Start Soon

It's difficult to overestimate the importance of an early start on saving toward a goal, whatever that goal is. Here, something called the "rule of 72" comes into play. This mathematical rule says that the time it takes a quantity to double equals 72 divided by the growth rate:

Doubling Time = 72/Growth Rate

This applies to any constantly growing quantity, but it's striking when applied to money. If a sum of money is growing at 7 percent a year, that money will double in about ten years. If you have an amount you want to reach in ten years, you only have to save half that amount today. If you want to reach that amount in twenty years, you have to save only one-fourth of that amount today. That amount will double once, then double again, and you'll have reached your goal.

The longer you wait before starting to save for a goal, the less time that the Rule of 72 has to do its work. So start early.

Get It Out of Sight

However you choose to save, it is important to get it out of sight. That is, get the money to someplace where you can't easily see it.

I know someone who opened a savings account at an inconvenient credit union with only one branch. Parking was always iffy at that credit union because it was located in the middle of a big university hospital complex. Why the deliberate seeking out of inconvenience? Because that was his way of getting the money out of sight. If he had an impulse to spend some from those savings, he'd face the hassle of getting the money out. He tricked himself into doing the right thing.

Maybe you won't have to go to such lengths to keep from spending your savings. Whatever it takes, though, do it! If you let that money stay in your checking account or your pocket, intending to save it at the end of the month, you may end up spending it.

This is another place where the power of bounded frittering can work for you. If you have $200 in checking that you'd like to move to savings, but you just can't make yourself do it, then deposit $175 of it in savings right away, pulling $25 to indulge yourself on some little treat.

Saving for a House

If you're going to be in an area for a while and want to settle down, buying a house can be a smart move. It was once rock-solid advice to buy a house because of the near-certain increases in the value of real estate. The advice is no longer as solid, but it is still good advice for those who are not going to be moving for a while.

The best home loans are available when you have a substantial down payment, 20 percent or more of the purchase price. There are also closing costs to pay. Saving up a down payment and closing costs was once a considerable obstacle in the way of would-be homeowners.

Today, there are many "no-down" and "low-down" loan programs, especially for first-time home buyers. If you very much want to own a home and you have a steady job, you probably can. It's important, however, to match your income and your expectations. Sometimes young people want to buy a house just like the one they moved out of when they left home. Often that's not possible, because the house they left was the product of many years of their parents' work in careers, and they're starting out—naturally enough—in an entry-level job.

Still, the best loans are available for those who have saved. Most people saving to buy a house will be best off keeping their money in a money market fund. They typically have a time horizon of five years or under, and the stock market is just too uncertain for so short a time horizon. True, there have been times when an investor could boost a potential down payment 50 percent just by keeping the money in stocks while waiting to buy a house. There have also been times when people were frozen out of a house because they were keeping the money in stocks that went down.

Saving for a Car

Many people save to buy a car. Earlier we saw the guideline that says you shouldn't buy a car if it takes a loan longer than three years to pay for it. It's a lot better, for many people, to save up and pay cash. That makes you the recipient of interest rather than the payer of interest. On the down side, you have to wait to get the car.

Interest is the price of waiting, as the quotation at the beginning of the chapter pointed out. You can receive that price or pay that price, depending on whether you wait or buy now. Whatever you do, choose a car carefully so you get the right one. It's awfully expensive to buy a car, decide you don't like it and turn around after a short time to buy something else.

Saving for "College"

Many people talk about saving for "college," but there may be a better way to express the thought. What you want to save up is a "future fund." It's a fund designed to promote the well-being of a young person, whatever that person's future holds.

For many people, that will be a four-year degree at a college or university. It's a good way to spend four years, and it prepares people for successful careers in a lot of different ways.

For many other people, college education isn't appropriate—and for a variety of good reasons. Some people want to do jobs for which a college education isn't appropriate. Technical or vocational training might be better. Other people would like to start a business or begin work as an independent contractor. For that matter, there are many jobs in our economy that don't require a college education—and yet are filled by college graduates because there aren't enough jobs around that require a college education.

The earlier a "future fund" is started, the better. More time gives the money a chance to grow. Given the seventeen-year time horizon for a newborn's future fund, most of the money should be invested in stock index funds, with their impressive long-term track record. At the time a future fund is started, the person who will benefit from the fund is in diapers, so it's not a good time to try to plan out that person's education, career and life.

Prepaid Tuition Programs

The rules for a general future fund are pretty simple. Start investing early, put the money primarily in stock index funds and leave it alone while it grows. Then, five years before the money is to be withdrawn, start shifting it out of stocks and toward a money market fund. Finally, write checks directly from the money market fund to pay bills that arise from college, technical training and the like.

Increasingly, however, there are vehicles for saving directly for college tuition. These prepaid tuition plans allow you to pay in advance for part or all of an education at a college or university. Because these plans take advantage of the ability of invested money to grow, you pay much less now than you would if you were enrolling someone in the college or university today.

These plans are usually a good idea, subject to one main qualification: it's important to check into what happens if you end up not enrolling your student in any of the schools covered by the plan. Why could this happen?

☐ The student might decide to go to a school outside the plan's coverage.

☐ The student might decide not to go to college at all.

☐ The student might not be eligible for admission to a college or university covered by the plan.

Some prepaid tuition plans impose penalties if you take the money out. Some return your money with interest, but the interest is set at a low level. Making a good decision typically involves estimating the chances that the student will go to one of the colleges and universities covered by the plan you consider.

Subject to that one qualification, prepaid tuition plans are excellent. They enjoy a favored tax status and they enable you to lock in tuition rates, which have been increasing faster than many other prices in recent years.

Saving up to pay for a young person's education is a great thing to do. More important, however, is instilling proper moral and religious values in that young person. Colleges and universities are, in some ways, dangerous places to be. Many students have failed to succeed in college because of drinking problems, drug addictions and the consequences of relationships. Few students have failed to succeed because of lack of money. Oh, there are plenty who have had to drop out for a while or take jobs to get the money to continue. But very few determined students have failed to complete a degree because money was the deciding obstacle.

Many parents wish there were some magic wand they could wave or some sacrifice they could make that would guarantee that their children reached the end of high school with strong moral and religious values. Unfortunately, there are no guarantees; parents can only do their best, with God's help, and then commit their children to God's care.

What Not to Do

Parents or other relatives sometimes get the idea of saving up a fund that will go to a child at a certain age, such as eighteen. They intend that the money will be used for college expenses, but if that's not spelled out, the money will become that person's property. It can then be used in any way that the beneficiary wants. This is usually a bad idea.

Often at age eighteen a student is not well equipped to make big life decisions. Blowing money that was intended for college is a big life decision, whether or not that fact is fully appreciated at the time.

Sometimes we don't do our best until we're challenged. In that sense it's not a good idea to present a student, no matter how diligent, with a college education on a platter. In my view it's far better to set up a cost-sharing arrangement, in which a student will have partial responsibility for covering college expenses. In my teaching at colleges and universities I have found that students are more mature and focused in their studies if they have at least partial responsibility for paying for their education.

Group Study Activities and Questions

1. Fill in the blanks of the following sentence: If I had it to do over again, the three things I would change about my education would be (1) _____ , (2) _____ and (3) _____ . Share your responses with the rest of the group, as they share theirs with you.

a. Do most members of the group wish they had more education or less education?

b. Is there anyone in the group who answered, "I would have studied less and partied more"?

c. Is there anyone in the group who answered, "I would have saved less money to pay for education"?

2. If you were going to make a down payment on a house four years from now, how comfortable would you be about leaving that money in the stock market until then? Why?

3. Does the year that occurs between each birthday you celebrate seem to be shorter now than when you were younger? Why do you think this is? Is it related to Psalm 39:4-5?

4. Does Matthew 6:31-34 teach us not to seek food or clothing at all? Should we just sit back waiting for it to fall out of the sky? If not, what does Matthew 6:31-34 teach about providing for ourselves?

5. If you had been given several thousand dollars to spend any way you wanted when you were eighteen, do you think you would have made wise decisions? Why or why not? What does this say about the advisability of saving for young people and presenting them with cash?

6. During the process of saving up to buy a home, is money spent on rent "thrown away"? Why or why not? Does this argue for trying to buy a home before you're ready?

11

Personal Finance for Youth

Teach your children well.
GRAHAM NASH

IN MANY HOUSEHOLDS A LOT OF THE ISSUES that come up for discussion, or even argument, involve young people and money. That's only natural. When we're talking about money, we're also talking about how we spend our time and resources.

These discussions can be much more productive and pleasant, and kids can grow up with a better attitude toward money, if they are taught money management beginning at an early age. This is a subject that's dear to me. For years I've been working with school-teachers as they integrate economics, personal finance and money management into what they're teaching. I have been impressed with what students can learn if they're only taught.

I have also been impressed with how badly students can do with money if they're not exposed to sound teaching. It's easy for young men and women to get off to a bad start in their financial lives. All it takes is a few enticing credit card applications, a little too much charging early on, and someone just out of school can be contemplating bankruptcy. Let's have a look at how this can be avoided, starting when kids are still quite young.

The Bible advises us to love God with all our heart, soul and strength (Deuteronomy 6:5). Then it adds: "These commandments that I give you today are to be upon your hearts. Impress them on your children. Talk about them when you sit at home and when you walk along the road, when you lie down and when you get up" (Deuteronomy 6:6-7).

Clearly the mandate to parents is to make God's commandments part of everyday life. This is far more important than education about money management—so if there arises a conflict between the two, there's no doubt which has to give way.

The Release Curve

Experts in child development sometimes talk about the transition to independence in terms of a "release curve." It's a graph that shows how children can be given more and more responsibility for themselves, until the time when they're released to be adults on their own. Figure 11.1 shows how it works in an ideal situation.

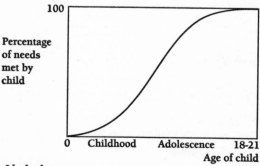

Figure 11.1. Ideal release curve

At the far left, the graph shows that a newborn baby takes 0 percent responsibility. The parents are 100 percent responsible for the baby's well-being. As the baby becomes a toddler and a child, the parents can leave more to the child. Kids learn to fix a snack from the refrigerator instead of getting someone else to do it for them. As adolescence approaches, the child carries more and more responsibility. Finally (often in the late teens) the child is released from the home.

The smooth, idealized release curve shows the general idea: more and more responsibility as the years go by. In practice, of course, the curve is not so smooth. There will be bumps in the curve where a child takes more responsibility—for example, when a child starts school. There will be other bumps when the child spends time away from home at summer camp or begins to make independent decisions about what courses to take in high school. For many households, the release curve will be bumpier (see figure 11.2).

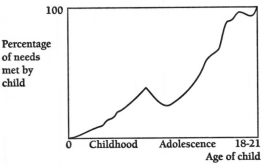

Figure 11.2. Typical release curve

What you don't want is a flat release curve—in which no more responsibility is transferred for months or years—followed by a major bump. You don't want children suddenly given responsibility without having been prepared for it.

As a university professor, I have seen many first-year students who weren't given enough responsibility at home. They often find the transition to university life difficult. From an environment where

Mom or Dad always bought the food, washed the clothes and made them do their homework, they have moved into an environment of great freedom. Suddenly they have to deal with dining plan decisions, balky coin-operated washing machines and the need to make themselves do their studying. Similar bumpy transitions occur for other young people pursuing different paths when they first leave home.

The Guiding Principle: Scarcity

Economists spend a lot of time working with the principle of scarcity, or the inability to satisfy all wants at the same time. Adults are familiar with scarcity because every day they have to make tradeoffs among their varied wants. Also, it's easy for even very young students to memorize the definition of scarcity.

What's difficult is getting children to truly understand the principle of scarcity. Here's why: They live in an environment where adults anticipate their needs and many of their wants. Any seeming shortages or scarcities are quickly and easily resolved by adults, from their point of view. If there's no milk in the refrigerator, one of the adults stops by the convenience store or the grocery store. Scarcity? No problem.

Children can't really understand scarcity until they've had to make decisions that involve choosing one good thing and giving up another good thing. The challenge for parents is to provide for their children's needs while teaching them how to deal with scarcity.

Understand in advance that if this is your job, you won't be perfect at it. You will sometimes give a child too much leeway and sometimes too little. But if you do nothing about teaching scarcity, if you continually provide for a child's needs and wants, you'll do that young person a great disservice. So don't wait until you come up with the absolute best way of teaching a child. Start sooner with something that's imperfect. But do start.

How to Start: Basic Choices

The first choices that young people make may not even involve money, but they're important choices. The grocery store is a good place to start, sometimes when kids are still young enough to be riding in the shopping cart. The choices will come up naturally enough. Kids learn quickly that by asking for a treat or snack as they pass it in the grocery aisle, they can often get it put into the cart. Here's where it is important for parents to look at the behavior they're rewarding. If kids get lots of snacks and treats by asking, they'll ask. If they get lots of snacks and treats by kicking and screaming, they'll kick and scream.

This is the time to set up a "one special treat" rule. Think about how often your grocery budget can stand a special treat and how much the treat can cost. Then tell the child, "You may have one special treat of your choice, and it has to be under $2." Notice how this introduces scarcity into the equation. The child now knows: *If I pick the cookies, I won't get the candy.* The child faces the inability to satisfy all wants at the same time. The child also gets some practice in reading the shelf numbers to know when something fits within the $2 limit and when it doesn't.

As a side benefit, this practice can make shopping trips less contentious. Instead of an endless series of grabs for snacks and treats, there's an opportunity for decision making. Especially for younger children, the parent will sometimes have to repeat the rules of the game—kids typically want both the candy and the cookies!

Note two further points about this exercise. First, it's vital that you stick to the rules you outline. If a child learns that whining can make one treat into three or four, the exercise won't work. Second, this exercise won't work with every child. If the child isn't ready to understand the rules, or if she is not mature enough to make a decision, then giving the choice will just be frustrating.

Above all, remember the point: to get a child to learn firsthand what scarcity is. A child can't fully understand what it means to trade off wants if his every want is always satisfied.

Allowance: The Two-Part Solution

It's common for parents to provide their children with an allowance. The size and nature of the allowance, though, can be points of contention. That's why I recommend a two-part solution.

Under this plan, the allowance consists of two parts. One part is a small but regularly paid sum. The second part is compensation for some household tasks as mutually agreed on.

There are other ways to do it, but in my view this way is the most economically sound.

Some parents simply respond to a child's reported "needs," giving money for each "need." The problem here is that the child never faces scarcity, learning instead that the way to get things is to ask for them (and later to whine, bully or threaten to get them).

Other parents insist that every penny of the allowance be earned. Although this is good for promoting a work ethic, it causes problems when there are fluctuations in the household's money-earning opportunities. For example, a child might want to save extra money for spending on a school field trip at a time when not much household work is available. It's possible to be hard-nosed about this and lecture the child: "You should have saved up earlier." But the lecture may not have the intended effect.

Another problem with insisting that every penny of allowance be earned is this: it implies that things are done in the household only to earn money. There are things that need to be done in every household, and the adults have the right to insist that kids do those chores unpaid. Otherwise, any request in the household might be met with the query "What will you pay me for it?"

It's important to consider what items are to be accounted for by the allowance. Giving a child too much responsibility too early is almost as bad a mistake as giving too little. For example, giving an allowance that seems sufficient to cover school expenses, and then insisting that the child cover all those expenses, is not a good idea for most elementary school children. They may find themselves needing a notebook or some replacement markers, having spent all their money. Ordinarily, discovering the consequences of overspending would be a useful part of the exercise, but you don't want a child penalized in school for the sake of this lesson. That's especially true for younger children.

What's important is making sure you don't reward the wrong things. If you lay down the law about how much allowance you will give but later cover an expense that was supposed to have been covered by allowance, you teach overspending.

The Importance of Allowing Mistakes

Parents have a natural tendency to shield their children from mistakes. This is a tendency that they have to resist in order to teach financial responsibility. Sure, parents will bail their kids out of some mistakes. If all mistakes are immediately corrected by a parent, though, little learning will take place.

A child may save up and want to buy a toy that the parent can clearly see won't last long. At some point the parent has to allow the purchase—and the consequences.

An older child may be spending money during a vacation at a pace that will exhaust the funds before the vacation is over. At some point the parent has to let the consequences sink in.

Youth groups provide good opportunities for teaching responsibility in stages. Sports teams, scouting units or church groups that take trips can provide important side benefits in teaching financial responsibility. On these trips youth must manage their money, often without Mom or Dad there. Typically the youth leader or peers will bail out kids who make mistakes like spending lunch money playing arcade games—but under circumstances that help teach a lesson.

It's also important for kids to learn the power of "bounded frittering." Consider what happens if they learn that it's OK for them to spend everything in the piggy bank and that Mom or Dad will then bail them out. That's a bad habit. It is far better for kids to learn that, within their saving and spending plan, they can take out a limited amount of money but then spend it any way they want.

Some mistakes are so serious that the parent may have to intervene. An excess of credit card debt in a teenager's life may be one example. Continuing credit card balances are financial poison. Just consider the following illustration: If an eighteen-year-old borrowed $1,000 every year on a credit card at 18 percent and never paid the balance down, how high would the total get by age sixty-five? The answer is $15,664,258.59!

> No matter how many times we hear the story of the prodigal son (Luke 15:11-32), there's always something new to learn from it. A son asks for his inheritance ahead of time. He's about to make a big mistake; he ends up squandering the money in wild living. But at that point his father doesn't stop him from making the mistake. Instead he lets his son go and stands by, ready to welcome his son back when he returns, repentant.
>
> Sometimes that's what parents have to do with their children: let them make their own mistakes, no matter how painful. Equally, they need to be ready to help when children experience the consequences of those mistakes and turn back.

Jobs: In the Household and Beyond

Under a two-part allowance scheme, part of the allowance is regularly doled out and the other part is earned. The part that's earned is important. It teaches the rewards of work and it teaches scarcity. Remember that in a child's world it's hard even to see that scarcity exists if a parent is always taking care of every need.

The main mistakes to avoid here are overpaying and underpaying for household work. If you overpay, you give a child an unrealistic idea of how easy it is to make money in the wider world. This can lead to discouragement, as when a teenager takes his or her first real job and finds out that vastly more perseverance is required to earn real money.

If you underpay for household work, you may artificially discourage a child from working. Part of the function of paid household jobs is to help children see the benefit of working. Putting these ideas together, I recommend an hourly rate for kids from twelve to sixteen years old that's somewhere between 50 and 100 percent of the minimum wage. When a sixteen-year-old is considering a real job outside the home, that sixteen-year-old should have a realistic idea of how difficult it is to find work that will be worth the minimum wage to an employer.

It's easy to see the advantages to teenagers in working outside the home. The teenager is exposed to the world of work, gets an independent source of spending money and begins to take more responsibility. The disadvantages, in my view, are more subtle. They include time spent away from studies and extracurricular activities, along with the reduction in safety that can come from working the hours involved with some jobs.

This is a decision for each involved household to make. My own impression is that there are many families that wish they had restricted the work hours of their teenagers or had them start part-time jobs later in the high school years. There are only a few, in my experience, that wish they had gotten their teenagers into part-time jobs sooner.

What's Taught in School

You may get some help in teaching financial responsibility by what's taught in the schools. Increasingly, economic education is part of the curriculum. The National Council on Economic Education offers excellent materials that are being used in many school systems. Further, many school systems are adopting competencies in economics and personal finance as learning objectives.

Sometimes model societies are formed in classrooms. The best known of these programs is the Mini-Society. In these model societies students form companies and sell products to each other to learn about economics and entrepreneurship. These programs are good as far as they go. Sometimes, however, the young participants get so much help from parents that the simulation doesn't do a good job of teaching scarcity.

Another popular teaching tool is a stock market simulation. In such simulations students are given hypothetical computer money, and they buy and sell stocks in an effort to get a high portfolio value. The best known of these is the Stock Market Game, sponsored by the Securities Industry Foundation for Economic Education.

I have done quite a bit of research on this game and have discovered that some teachers do a great job with it. In other classrooms, however, students learn the wrong lessons. By practicing short-run trading, they get the idea that trading stocks would be a good idea with their own money when they get out of school. Buying and holding index funds would be a much better idea. In fairness, the game materials do not encourage speculation with real money—but then, they don't adequately point out the advantages of buying stock funds (as opposed to buying individual stocks).

Sometimes people get the idea that economic education is intended to make students more greedy or acquisitive—to make them into little tycoons. There's always good-natured laughter when a fifth-grader talks about making money in a stock market game by short selling. To me, that's not what economic education should be doing. By teaching the principles of scarcity and choice, economic education should make students more oriented toward making good decisions—but not necessarily more acquisitive.

Although schools may help students learn financial responsibility, that job will ultimately fall back on the parents. Particularly by example, parents will have a strong effect on how children view money and ultimately use it.

The Special Case of Holidays

Some of the biggest family tensions about finances come up in connection with the holiday season in December. Kids' expectations can run high, no matter what their age. For the younger set, those expectations will often include toys heavily advertised on TV. Teenagers will have different expectations, often centered on holiday times with their friends. Most of these expectations involve money—sometimes lots of it.

It's a mistake to get trapped into spending too much at holiday time. Some families spend so much that they're still paying the bills after summer heat has replaced December cold. This sets a bad example of money management for the kids.

In economics the law of diminishing marginal utility shows us how people don't value additional units of a good as much as they valued the first few units. An ice cream cone is great on a hot day. A second one is still pretty good. But a third or fourth ice cream cone wouldn't add much to our happiness.

While this law applies to adults, it applies with special force to small children at holiday time when they are showered with presents. The first few presents are awesome, the next few are great—but then, pretty soon, it doesn't make much difference to the child whether there are ten or twelve presents.

All this suggests that it's not worthwhile to stretch your budget to spend more on the holidays. I once wrote a column for the *Wall Street Journal* having a little fun with excessive holiday spending. In the column I proposed splitting off the religious aspects of the holiday and calling what was left "Excessmas." This would be a holiday devoted to excess in spending, eating and drinking. My column hit a responsive note, and I received messages from across the country confirming the sentiment. Clearly a lot of people thought that holiday spending had gone to excess.

Any time of the year is good for teaching financial responsibility. The holidays are an especially good time because the season is not about spending money.

 The idea for my column on Excessmas came to me following a candlelight Christmas Eve service at my church, Beaver Creek Church of the Brethren. This quiet and inspirational service was special for me and for my family. But that same Christmas season was labeled as "dismal" in the business press because retail sales had not achieved expectations. The contrast between our joyous Christmas and the "dismal Christmas" of the business press firmly convinced me that we needed to do something to separate the commercial holiday from the religious one. Humor can be a powerful weapon; in this case, I was trying to get all of us to laugh at ourselves for the extent to which we had turned the holiday season into "Excessmas."

Group Study Activities and Questions

1. Describe your favorite Christmas—that is, the Christmas observance you cherish the most in memory. Listen as the other members of your group describe their favorite Christmases.

a. Was your favorite Christmas from your childhood or from sometime later?

b. What part did the observance of Christ's birth play in that holiday?

c. Of what importance was the amount of money spent on that holiday?

2. What is, or was, your "release curve" like? Did you smoothly go from 100 percent to 0 percent reliance on your parents? Have you been released yet? Was the curve bumpy rather than smooth, with big changes in your responsibility and freedom in a short time?

3. Some writers believe that children understand less about scarcity now than their parents did when they were growing up. Is it true? If so, what's the reason—kids' attitudes, their knowledge or just a general increase in wealth?

4. Read the parable of the prodigal son (Luke 15:11-32). Would it have been OK for the father to have told the son, "No, I'm not giving you your inheritance. Now be quiet and get back to work"? What might have happened then? More generally, under what conditions should a parent intervene to save a child from the consequences of a poor choice?

5. Why is it a mistake to pay too much for household work done by a child? Why is it a mistake to pay too little?

6. Deuteronomy 6:7 calls on parents to teach their children God's commandments throughout daily life: "when you sit at home and when you walk along the road, when you lie down and when you get up." What would be the corresponding description of the times that parents interact with their children today? Is the job of teaching children the faith easier or more difficult than it was in Old Testament times?

Merry Excessmas!
Reprinted from the Wall Street Journal

Christmas means different things to different people. The dominant culture views it as a commercial holiday—a time when stores ring up record sales, people use inoffensive and nonsectarian greetings such as "Happy holidays," and some even file lawsuits to prevent Nativity scenes from going up at government buildings.

But there is also a large religious minority that chafes at the commercial and religiously sanitized nature of the holiday. Some of these believers react by trying to make the holiday more religious and more sectarian; as the shopping bag from the Christian bookstore says: "Jesus is the Reason for the Season." In a religiously diverse society, however, this approach is bound to fail.

Therefore I propose a different approach: Let us split what is now known as Christmas into two holidays. The first holiday would be called Nativity, and it would be exclusively religious. Christians would celebrate this holiday, with no expectation that the government or people of other faiths would recognize it. The second holiday is harder to name, but for now let's call it Excessmas. This holiday would be the season associated with excess in everything, including promotion, spending, consuming and drinking.

Splitting the holiday would have a number of advantages. First, it would increase the precision of language in economic reporting. If retail sales lag projections, the media commonly report that it is a "dismal Christmas." What's dismal in that case is actually Excessmas. Christmas—as Nativity—could be more joyful than ever in such a season. The sales associated with Nativity are small: fourth-quarter sales associated with Excessmas are a very important economic phenomenon.

Second, it would improve holiday observances. Christians would celebrate Nativity and Jews, of course, would continue to celebrate Hanukkah. Both groups could withdraw from celebrating Excessmas. Religious observances would be purely religious, with no thought of toning them down for the sake of pluralism. Meanwhile, Excessmas parties would no longer be encumbered with a fuzzy need to do something unselfish or feel warm feelings. They could be wholly devoted to excess.

Third, it would solve the perennial Nativity-scene debate. Churches would set up Nativity scenes on their own property, where, we all agree, purely religious expressions are celebrated (and constitutionally protected). Governments would put up Excessmas lights on utility poles and malls would set up Excessmas displays to promote retail spending.

Fourth, it would reduce holiday stress and depression. The holiday blues are a common occurrence, partly attributed to the futile quest for a "perfect Christmas." The food must be perfect, the fire in the fireplace must burn brightly, and there really ought to be snow falling (even though the majority of our population lives where that's statistically rare). That's a perfect Excessmas, not a perfect

Nativity. A perfect celebration of excess isn't needed. All it has to be is excessive.

Meanwhile, the celebrants of Nativity would find their perfection in what's being celebrated and not in their own activities. Splitting the holiday could greatly reduce the disappointment of unfulfilled expectations.

And finally, it would end uncomfortable feelings that the season lasts too long. Nativity would be a short holiday appropriate to the religious observance. Excessmas, devoted as it is to excess in everything, could begin with September catalog mailings (as it does now) or even earlier.

If we split Nativity from Excessmas, we would only be recognizing what has long been fact for many observances. When the school chorus sings the praises of shoppers hearing silver bells or the jolly figure who's coming to town with his full toy bag, the connection is to Excessmas, not Nativity. When the office party is made innocuous to religious sensibilities, the main principle it celebrates is indulgence. (Not that I would deny others their indulgences. I'm a teetotaler, not a prohibitionist.)

The December 25 origin of Christmas, we are told, was that early Christians wanted to celebrate at a time when the surrounding pagan revelries would cover their celebration. They rightly feared persecution and did not want to be conspicuous. Times have changed, but splitting the holiday would bring Christians back to their roots. It would allow for more precise reporting and an honest recognition of what's being celebrated during Nativity and Excessmas.

12

Retirement

Money may kindle, but it cannot by itself,
and for very long, burn.
IGOR STRAVINSKI

S TRAVINSKI GOT IT RIGHT, DIDN'T HE? Money can't burn by itself, and it can't burn very long. Although saving for retirement is an important financial goal, strangely enough there are plenty of retired people who have a lot of money but not much happiness. Avoiding an unhappy retirement involves making investments earlier in life, both of money and of time. We'll see how both kinds of investments can pay off in the retirement years.

To a great degree, your happiness in retirement will depend more on not worrying than on the amount of money you'll have. I advise a retired couple of modest means. They're happy because they don't worry. It's part of their overall outlook on life. I also know other retired people with more money than they have time to spend on things they want. That money hasn't bought them security, though, because they spend time worrying.

How can we tell senior citizens "Don't worry" when they're facing everything that comes along with growing old? That assurance comes from God.

The righteous will flourish like a palm tree,
  they will grow like a cedar of Lebanon;
planted in the house of the LORD,
  they will flourish in the courts of our God.
They will still bear fruit in old age,
  they will stay fresh and green,
proclaiming, "The LORD is upright;
  he is my Rock, and there is no wickedness in him." (Psalm 92:12-15)

This is not to take lightly the declining physical health and other worries that often come with old age. It is instead to recognize that God is in control. God has the ability to give us good gifts when we ask, even more than earthly parents have the ability to give good gifts to their own children (Matthew 7:11).

Reducing Worries: The Role of Social Security

Much has been written about the financial future of government-run retirement programs such as Social Security in the United States. These government-run programs don't invest money in accounts that correspond to individual retirement accounts. Instead for the most part they're transfer programs that tax current wage earners to pay current retirees.

It's easy to see why some people think otherwise. Social Security in the United States is set up to look like an insurance program. The Social Security card says, "This number has been established for [the recipient]." Social Security brochures refer to the taxes you have to pay as "contributions." The fact is, however, that Social Security today is a tax-and-transfer program. In return for your Social Security taxes paid in, you get an implicit promise that future generations will tax themselves to pay you Social Security when you retire.

A skeptic once said, "An implicit promise isn't worth the paper it's written on." Obviously he was joking, since an implicit promise isn't written at all! Social Security is highly popular politically, so there's every reason to believe that it will be there, especially for low-income retirees, in the future. So the first step in not worrying about retirement security is realizing that you won't starve in the streets, because of Social Security. Whether you'll get substantial benefits, or benefits appropriate to your level of "contributions" over the years, is another story.

Reducing Worries: Stay the Course

It would also be worrisome if retirement required a substantial change in investment strategy, especially more active management of your investments. You can rest easy about that. Just as "buy and hold index funds" was the best strategy for accumulating wealth, so "hold and sell index funds" is the best strategy for getting the money out as you need it.

Both elements of "hold and sell" are important. The "hold" part means that you don't convert all your investments into cash on the day you retire. The same considerations that call for holding diverse investments all along continue after retirement. The "sell" part means that you sell part of your investments as you need the money. Often this is done automatically for you. For example, money that has been tax-sheltered, as in a 401(k) account, will be returned to you according to a procedure set by law. The year after you turn seventy and a half years old, you're required to start taking minimum distributions from those accounts. The amount is recalculated each year based on your life expectancy.

Retirement is no reason to start tracking the value of investments daily, switching funds around and chasing the highest yields. Remember, that's a counterproductive strategy anyway.

Reducing Worries: Ease into Bonds

Stocks are risky in the short term and bonds are less so. For the young person saving for retirement forty-plus years down the road, the superior long-run returns from stock funds call for a heavy commitment to these funds. Many savvy investors, as we have seen, believe that low-cost index funds are the best way to invest in stocks over the long run.

As retirement approaches, worries can be eased by gradually changing the allocation between stocks and bonds. No big moves are necessary. For many people approaching retirement, a simple reallocation of new contributions to retirement programs will be sufficient. Someone who was contributing 50-50 to stock and bond funds, for example, might go to 40-60 or so—but only with new contributions. That would leave money previously invested where it was. The new money going in would be tilted toward bond funds.

What are the risks we're dealing with, anyway? The risk faced by someone who has retired holding stock funds and bond funds is this: the stock market may go down and stay down for a period of years before resuming growth. That down period wouldn't be a good time to be selling stocks. Having holdings of bond funds would provide the income to get through until the stock funds come back.

So why not go entirely to bond funds if they're less risky? The answer consists of good news and bad news. The good news is that retirees are living longer, healthier lives. Advances in medical care permit vigorous and enjoyable lifestyles in retirement. The bad news is that retirees are living so long that it's possible for them to outlive their money if it doesn't keep growing. So even retirees need the greater long-run growth potential of stocks in their portfolios. Further, living a long time increases the probability of living through a period of sharp inflation, when there is a general increase in all prices. Stocks do better than bonds in preserving your purchasing power in a time of inflation.

All this explains why easing toward bonds in portfolio allocations is a low-worry strategy for retirement. The sensible strategy is not a sudden or massive shift but a gentle shift over time. You could do worse than to follow the age-percent rule introduced in an earlier chapter, moving about one percentage point more toward bonds each year of retirement. For many people, that can be easily accomplished by selling more stocks than bonds in a given year as they make withdrawals from their retirement funds.

Reducing Worry: Really Safe Investments

I have held for last two forms of really safe investments: TIPS and annuities.

TIPS stands for "Treasury Inflation-Protected Securities." They're an especially safe kind of U.S. government bond. They have been around since 1997, and they promise to pay you back your principal plus interest plus an additional amount for inflation that has occurred during the life of the bond. Therefore, if the inflation rate took off, you would receive a lot of money.

TIPS come close to guaranteeing you a "real" rate of return. Economists distinguish between the "nominal rate" of return (before correction for inflation) and the "real rate" (after a correction for inflation). The distinction is important. If I told you I had government bonds that pay you 30 percent a year, would you be interested? (Probably so.) If I told you those 30 percent government bonds were issued by a foreign government with an inflation problem, would you still be interested? (Probably not, since the real return might be low or nonexistent.)

If you're worried about the security of retirement income, then, you can put part of your holdings into TIPS. Remember, though, that you should still have some stock funds for long-term growth.

Another useful asset to have in retirement is an annuity. Generally speaking, an annuity is any regular stream of payments. The most useful kind of annuity for a retiree is a lifetime benefit. Here's how it works: You pay up-front for the annuity, and in return the issuer promises you a fixed payment for life. The issuer is making similar contracts with other people and pooling the risk. Some people will live out a long life, collecting that fixed payment for a long time. Other people won't, while still other people will come in close to the average. The issuer of the annuity is pooling risks so that individuals can receive a guaranteed income for life.

You should make use (limited use) of annuities as a risk-reduction device. Many retirement plans will offer you the possibility of a one- or two-lifetime arrangement at retirement. Under the two-lifetime arrangement, a surviving spouse will continue to receive payments for life.

A worry-free retirement income scheme could therefore start with Social Security, build from there with a small annuity, and from there include a mix of stock funds and bond funds. The mix of stock and bond funds would gradually move more toward bonds over time. Don't worry about getting the mix of stock and bond funds just right either. A good allocation scheme will gradually move you in the direction of bonds. If you spend time worrying about the perfect allocation scheme and don't move any money until you're sure you've got it right, you may end up doing nothing. That would leave you heavy with stock funds.

Investments of Time, Not Just Money

We have been concentrating on the investments of money that can lead to a financially secure retirement. Equally important are the investments of time. Someone once said that the purpose of education is to be interesting company, even when you're alone. You'll be more interesting company to yourself in retirement if you invest time before retirement.

Fortunately, most of these investments are pleasant. They include building relationships with family (especially grown children) and friends. They include developing interests in music, art, crafts, leisure sports—the kinds of things that make our lives richer and can be enjoyed at any age.

The most important investment of time a person can make is in knowing God through Jesus Christ. There are people who, assuming Christianity is a religion of rules, figure that they'll live fast and loose until they're old and then start following the rules. Sadly, they have missed the point. The fast-and-loose lifestyle is ultimately empty; Christ's grace is liberating. And there's always the tragedy of someone dying with only a future intention to seek God out.

All the same, if someone comes to God late in life, Christians have no right to regard that late convert with any less respect than any other believer. God is the Judge. If we gripe about God's generosity in this case, we're no better than the vineyard workers whom Jesus taught about. They came to work for a full day in the vineyard, worked in the hot sun and got a day's wages (a denarius coin). The vineyard's owner had gone out later, getting some workers so late that they worked only an hour—but they got a denarius too! The all-day workers complained, but the master of the vineyard explained that he wasn't being unfair to them. He gave them what they agreed to work for. The master concluded by asking, "Don't I have the right to do what I want with my own money? Or are you envious because I am generous?" (Matthew 20:15).

"Disconnecting" Versus "Easing Back"

Well before retirement, it's important to adopt a healthy attitude toward work and leisure. The "disconnecting" approach goes something like this: You hate your work but you work and save hard. You do useful work every waking minute and you cut back on sleep to make more waking minutes. You live where the opportunity is best, not where you would like to live. Then when you retire, you disconnect. You love doing nothing and you spend all your time doing nothing. You move to where you have always wanted to live and you live happily ever after, not doing anything for anybody.

The disconnecting approach seldom works. There are many things that can go wrong with it. If you hate your work but stay in it to pile up money during your working years, you may reduce your capacity for enjoying life. If you don't develop interests and hobbies, you may not be able to do so after retirement. If you move somewhere new, you may not like it there. If you do nothing useful for anyone else, you may lose the joy of living. Finally, if you have been used to a fast pace for years on end, you may find hammock time punishing.

If not the "disconnecting" approach, then what? The answer is the "easing back" approach. Under this approach, you position yourself over time to be in a career that you enjoy. Maybe you have to work hard and save at times, but you don't go back year after year to a job you hate. You don't try to do something useful in every waking minute, and you don't short yourself on sleep. You spend some time just doing nothing. You live where you want to live, all things taken together. You develop interests and hobbies and relationships with others.

Then when you retire, you ease back rather than disconnecting. You spend more of your time doing just what you want to do, but you don't end your connections with the community of humans around you. And while you aren't working a full-time job, you are spending some time doing things for other people. You don't have to move to some distant retirement paradise, because you're already in a place you like.

I have known people who assumed that they would love retirement because it would be so different from their working lives, which they loathed. They were wrong. Maybe you know some people like that. They show us that the best way to prepare for retirement—and enjoy career years—is to learn how to enjoy life before retirement.

Housing: Preserving Options

Housing during retirement is one of those areas where a little foresight can go a long way. When people get older, their housing needs and wants change. After the kids have left home, it's no longer so important to have a lot of room, and it's more important to have a house that's easily maintained and cleaned. Things like ease of entry into a house (without climbing steps) become important. The user-friendliness and accessibility of bathrooms can become a concern.

People make three avoidable mistakes that affect retirement housing:

□ *Buying or building a house that assumes eternal youth.* Some people, not many years away from retirement, move into rather inaccessible houses. Such houses might include multiple levels and steps, together with tiny bathrooms that make refitting for access difficult. In some cases the houses are on huge areas of land that require maintenance and mowing. Now, I'm not suggesting that everyone over thirty buy houses assuming that they'll be retirement houses. I'm only pointing out that, with a little foresight, decisions about retirement housing won't have to be made in a hurry.

□ *Being unwilling to hire help.* Some senior citizens are quite capable of living on their own, with only a little help on the more strenuous household chores. There are people with large portfolios of securities who are unwilling to pay the kid down the street to mow the lawn. They instead take it as some kind of great personal dishonor that they don't feel strong enough to care for the yard.

□ *Ruling out remodeling.* Frequently a house can be adapted to comfortable retirement living. Remodeling can improve approaches to entrances and improve accessibility of kitchens and bathrooms. Again, some senior citizens think there's something wrong with having this kind of remodeling done.

Some people tend to get their feeling of self-worth from their work. For such people, retirement can be traumatic. The biblical antidote to such feelings is the assurance of God's regard for every individual. Jesus said, "Are not five sparrows sold for two pennies? Yet not one of them is forgotten by God. Indeed, the very hairs of your head are all numbered. Don't be afraid; you are worth more than many sparrows" (Luke 12:6-7).

Group Study Activities and Questions

1. Complete the following sentence: On an ideal day after I retire, I would _____. Share your sentence with the rest of the group.

a. Do any of the answers include doing "work"?

b. Do the answers assume that you'll be in perfect health after retirement?

c. Do the answers assume that you'll have plenty of money after retirement?

2. Do you think you will ever receive Social Security? If you do, are you worried about the financial problems of Social Security? If you don't, do you believe that the older generation will silently stand by and let Social Security be abolished?

3. Do you currently have any hobbies or favorite activities that can be enjoyed by retirees? Do you currently have any hobbies or favorite activities that require you to be youthful to participate? Explain.

4. Have someone read the parable of the workers in the vineyard (Matthew 20:1-16). Why were the all-day workers upset with the master of the vineyard? Would you have been upset if you had been one of the all-day workers? How do you feel when you learn that a death row inmate has accepted Christ?

5. Sometimes people get offered buyouts that enable them to retire with full benefits at age fifty-five. Would such a buyout be attractive to you, or would you turn down such an offer? Why?

6. If you lived in your current residence until retirement, could it easily be adapted to the needs of an older resident? Did you think about any of this when buying it? If you did think about it, would that amount to worrying about tomorrow, as was advised against in Matthew 6:34?

13

For Those You Love

You can't take it with you.
You never see a U-Haul following a hearse.
ELLEN GLASGOW

IF I TOLD YOU THERE WAS SOMETHING you could do to help out those you love at a very difficult time, you'd want to do it, right? Well, there is something you can do. And it will be a tremendous help to all those you love. It involves planning for your own serious illness or death.

Did you react to that by saying, "Whoa, I'm outta here"? If so, that's understandable. People don't like to think about these things. To be sure, we shouldn't dwell on them. That's why I think we should take care of these matters and then forget about them. However, you should know this: if you *don't* take care of these matters, you'll be putting a big burden on those you love at a difficult time for them.

The Danger of "When in Doubt, Do More"

Treatment for serious illness and injuries generally operates according to the principle "When in doubt, do more." This means that when a patient is beyond hope of recovering a useful life, the tendency of the medical care system is still to try to keep that patient alive.

In itself, that's not bad. If a mistake has to be made, better that it should be a mistake in favor of extending life rather than cutting it off. Think about what would happen if the opposite were true. Then emergency room staff would be looking for a way to end the life of a patient rather than to preserve it!

The problem comes when medical treatment goes on and on. It can go well beyond what the patient would authorize if able to communicate. It can go well beyond what the patient has told family and friends. This is not something we talk about every day, but when we hear news reports about (for example) someone in a vegetative state being kept alive, it may come up in conversation. Most of us have heard a relative say, some time or another, "If I'm ever like that, you can pull the plug."

The problem, then, with "When in doubt, do more" is that it can drain family resources while going against the wishes of the patient. It can make decision making more difficult than would be the case if the patient's wishes were known. To avoid this, you have to make your wishes known. Here are the three steps in doing that:

☐ First, fill out an "advance medical directive" (AMD). This is a legal document that specifies how you want to be treated if you are ever in grave medical trouble.

☐ Second, fill out a "durable power of attorney." This is a legal document giving someone you trust the ability to specify how your case is to be treated if you are in a grave medical condition and unable to speak for yourself. Often the person you designate will be your spouse or a close relative.

☐ Third, let people know. Give your family doctor a copy of your advance medical directive and your durable power of attorney. Keep copies in your "important papers" drawer. Keep other copies in a safe-deposit box. Give copies to the person you named in your durable power of attorney. In an emergency it's surprising how hard it can be to locate these documents.

Once someone confidently told me that she would never be a drain on family resources because of extended medical treatment. She said that she'd just tell the doctors what she wanted. In talking further with her about this, however, I learned that she had not completed an advance medical directive or a durable power of attorney. Sadly, she might not be conscious at the time when she would want to convey these sentiments to the doctors. Without the right documents, her wishes might not be followed.

Keep in mind what happens if you casually say to relatives once in a period of years how you would want your medical treatment handled—but you never get the paperwork done. Then, if relatives do have to make decisions about your treatment, they'll be trying to remember what you said "last Thanksgiving" or "Christmas before last." You'll be making it unnecessarily hard on them. Remember, too, that if they're uncertain about your wishes, they'll fall back on "When in doubt, do more." They may keep your body technically alive much longer than there's any hope of recovery. They don't want to, but the uncertainty forces them to. They may also suffer from unnecessary guilt if they make a sensible decision that you would have approved—but you never let them know.

> For those who belong to Christ, it is not hard to sign an advance medical directive asking that life support be withdrawn when there is no hope of recovery. At such a time in the life of a Christian, the still-living body is only a barrier to heaven. Contemplating his own death, Paul wrote, "To me, to live is Christ and to die is gain" (Philippians 1:21). How much more this applies to a believer who has no hope of recovery in this world! Christians must understand, however, the terror of death that applies to those who do not have the hope that we have in Christ. For them, an advance medical directive specifies the end of all things good.

An Easy Rule: Have a Will

A will is a legal document in which you specify what should happen in the event of your death. Don't spend a lot of time thinking about whether you should have a will. Get one.

It's hard to say this strongly enough or often enough. If you're reading this book, you should have a will. If you're even serious enough about your personal finances to pick up a book like this, you should have a will. If you have any children, no matter what your age, you should have a will.

You may think that if you don't own much property, you don't need a will. But that assumes the will's primary purpose is to allocate your property after you're gone. That's only one thing a will accomplishes, and for many people, it's not the most important purpose.

For those who leave children behind, the most important purpose of the will is to provide for those children. Even if there's not a lot of property to divide, the will is the instrument by which a parent can let it be known who should be the guardians of the children. In the absence of a will the surviving family members will just have to guess. Would Uncle X and Aunt Y be good guardians? If not, then who?

For some people, the most important reason for getting a will is that it's part of a package that includes an advance medical directive and a durable power of attorney. If you have all this done at the same time, the cost is reasonable. Don't worry about it; just promise yourself this: *For the sake of those I love, I will get this legal work done.* Then go do it.

An Easy Rule: Use a Lawyer

Lots of people are amateur lawyers when it comes to wills. They confidently say things like "If I kick off, I know that all my property goes to my wife" or "I know it all goes to my husband and the kids." They might be right, but they might be wrong too. The law concerning wills differs from state to state. There are some unusual quirks, and with wills it's smart to pay an expert to steer you around the quirks. Things you'd assume from common sense don't always apply in the laws that deal with wills.

There are computer software packages that can draw up wills, along with documents like the advance medical directive and durable power of attorney. You just fill in the blanks and the computer does the rest. These software packages are OK for generic legal documents—so if that's the only way you'll do the documents, go ahead. You'd be better off using a lawyer, however.

When you're signing the documents generated by the computer, you're issuing some important instructions. If you rely only on the computer, you may not even understand what you're signing. A good lawyer can help you understand what the documents really do, beyond the legal language. Also, even after you sign the documents generated by a computer, there are requirements for filing and copies that differ by state.

In my state, for example, it's important to have the original will in a safe-deposit box and to have a copy in the home. If the bank burns and the will in the safe-deposit box is destroyed, then the copy in the home is valid—but the reverse isn't true. That's just one of the many quirks in the law from state to state.

While you're preparing wills and related documents, that's a good time to consider how well either spouse could deal with finances after the death of the other. In some households one spouse often makes all the financial decisions and keeps all the records. The loss of that spouse would leave the other in a difficult position. It's important that both spouses have a good idea of the household's finances, even if one or the other will specialize in paying the bills and making decisions most of the time

Last Instructions
We saw how "When in doubt, do more" applies in treating patients

who become the sudden victims of accident or illness. The medical system is tilted toward doing more, rather than doing less, if there's a doubt.

The funeral industry has the same tilt. That's not to say that funeral directors are crooks, but the tilt is there all the same. Those who have never planned or ordered a funeral find it hard to believe, but the number of decisions required is staggering. What kind of casket? What sort of memorial service? Where? What kinds of flowers? These are only a few of the questions.

In each case a great deal of money can be spent "doing more" rather than "doing less." The result is sometimes that much more is spent on a funeral than any member of the family would want, including the departed.

It's easy to understand how this comes about. The funeral seems to be the last chance to show love for the departed. It's hardly the time to scrimp. This is why the wishes of the departed can be a powerful influence on getting good decisions made.

The flowers of a funeral will wither and fade. The casket, over many years, will deteriorate. However, many kinds of memorials can last and last. In particular, memorial funds and scholarships perpetuate the memory of someone while helping people in the future. In the absence of instructions from the departed, there's a tilt toward such things as flowers and caskets—and away from memorial funds and scholarships, which take time and effort to set up. Once the funeral is over, people want to get on with their lives and not fret over the details of a memorial fund. That's why it's important that the funeral and memorial fund be specified in advance.

Forms are available for specifying funeral decisions in advance from funeral homes. When you specify a less costly alternative for your own funeral, there's no question of others inadvertently dishonoring you. You can make decisions about a funeral that others would feel uncomfortable making. Since their way of avoiding discomfort is often to go for the more expensive option, your advance directions can keep the cost within reasonable bounds. More importantly, you save them from an incredibly uncomfortable time of decision making.

You should know that making the decisions now doesn't require you to prepay for the funeral. Prepaid funeral plans vary quite a bit in their quality. Some are good, but others are extremely poor investments of your money. Unless you feel well qualified to evaluate the quality, it's better to make the decisions but skip paying for the funeral in advance.

One other important detail is this: Your funeral decisions need to be available in an accessible place in the event of your death. Among other things, this means:

☐ Those decisions should not be included in your will. Your will generally will not be read until sometime after your funeral.

☐ Those decisions should not be placed only in your safe-deposit box, if you have one. That box may be frozen at the time of your death, meaning that the contents will not be accessible until after the funeral.

☐ Those decisions should not be placed in a location where you're "sure" the family will look—without any further communication. After a death, especially an unexpected one, it's hard to predict where family members will look if they haven't been specifically told.

☼ Once a funeral director justified the expense of an ornate casket by saying it was a "jewel box" for something precious. Although a human life is precious, and dead bodies are to be treated with respect, Christians don't need to worry too much about preserving the physical body. We are assured that at the last day, God will give us new resurrection bodies that will live on forever (1 Corinthians 15:35-54). But in the meantime the earthly body decays, and no expenditure on caskets can change that fact. When you get right down to it, going to great lengths to preserve the body is pagan, not Christian.

Group Study Activities and Questions

1. Complete the following sentence: One thing I would want to happen at the time of my own funeral would be _____. Share your answers with the others in the group.

a. Based on funerals you know about, is your wish realistic, or is it unlikely to be fulfilled?

b. Is your wish more likely to be fulfilled if you communicate it in advance to relatives, or is it just one of those things that happens?

c. Does it spook you even to think about your own funeral? Do you think most people are that way?

2. Why do you think the general tendency of doctors is "When in doubt, do more"? Is that necessarily a bad thing when a doctor is dealing with the victim of a serious accident or illness?

3. Have someone read Philippians 1:21-26. (This was written by Paul from a jail cell in Philippi.) If you had been a personal friend of Paul and had read this in his letter, would you have been more worried or more encouraged about your friend's condition?

4. Would you consider filing a will that had been made up with a computer package? Would you consider letting a truck driver take out your appendix? What's the difference?

5. Why do you think funeral directors sometimes engage in the practice "When in doubt, do more"? Is it necessarily bad?

6. Why would it be a special matter of concern to an older person to determine what will happen to the wealth he or she has accumulated over a lifetime? Why would it be distressing "not knowing who will get it" (Psalm 39:6)?

Epilogue

Victorious Living in a Complex World

If you think you can win, you can win.
WILLIAM HAZLITT

W E HAVE COME TO THE END OF OUR JOURNEY toward simplifying our lives and honoring God with our finances. We first need to remember that in Jesus Christ we have a victory over the difficulties of this life. That victory is more important than any financial victory we could ever imagine. That victory is well worth remembering if we start to worry about finances.

Having dedicated ourselves and our resources to honoring God, we're in a position to celebrate a lesser victory, one that is important all the same: victory over worry and complication in our financial lives. When we abandon the goal of constructing the perfect financial plan, we free ourselves to prayerfully do some positive things about our finances.

For most people, there's a race going on between their wants and their means. As soon as they get a raise on the job—improving their finances—it turns out that their wants have expanded. The race is as close as ever, and they can't see any way to win the race but by getting more money. What if we stopped the race and refused to participate? Then we wouldn't find our wants always increasing ahead of our means.

Under this book's approach, we're no longer trying to track every penny of spending as we improve our monthly finances. Instead we're looking to find out where the money is going, to see that our spending is in line with our values. We're simplifying our lives by insuring against major insurable risks and then not worrying about them.

When we concentrate on honoring God and simplifying our lives with housing decisions, we concentrate on our needs rather than our wants, and we become comfortable with the idea of buying less housing than we can afford. In a similar way we buy a car or truck for transportation rather than to make a statement or soothe an old hurt. Along the way, we can ask whether we really want to live the hurried lifestyle that keeps us on the road when we might do better sharing time with family and friends.

In investing, giving up the struggle for the highest possible return leaves us free to choose durable investments that do well over time and don't require constant monitoring. Choosing a mix of assets neutralizes a lot of the risk. We aren't tempted to make the investment mistakes that come from greed and can end in disaster.

Honoring God and simplifying also help us be a positive influence on the youth in our lives. They are growing up in a society that tells them that more consumption and more spending is always better. We can help them see how shallow a life is when it's built on consuming more and spending more.

When we are secure in Christ, retirement and end-of-life decision making lose their terror. When we properly manage our resources, worry need not be a companion of retirement.

In my experience, most people have the ability to greatly improve their finances. All they're lacking is the confidence that they can do it. To these people, I would say, Try some of the exercises in this book. Go to chapter two and see how easy it is for Matt and Jan to spend less than they make, if they'll only sit down and do it. Then do the same thing with your budget. Or if your budget is in good shape, check out chapter six and see how easy it is to start putting money into good investments, a little bit at a time.

Nothing succeeds like success. If you can win a small victory or two in budgeting, you can go to the checklist in appendix two of this book and do a complete financial makeover. But remember the purpose of it all: not to accumulate wealth and then worry about it, but to honor God.

I hope that you have found this book helpful. It will be a measure of some success if you use plain and simple strategies to save and invest money. It will be a greater success if you find that you can worry less and put first things first, and Christ above all.

Appendix 1
Best Low-Cost Fund Provider

In investments, costs count, because they directly subtract from your investment return. That's why I recommend that you consider the Vanguard Group, which in my opinion is the best low-cost fund provider. Here is how to get in touch with them:

The Vanguard Group of Investment Companies
P.O. Box 2600
Valley Forge, PA 19482-2600
1-800-662-7447
www.vanguard.com

After this book is published, it's possible that someone will replace the Vanguard Group as the low-cost leader. If that happens, you'll find it on the *Getting a Grip on Your Money* website, <www.plainmoney.com>.

You should know that I am not an employee or consultant of the Vanguard Group. I have not been paid anything by the Vanguard Group for this endorsement. My only connection with the Vanguard Group is that I have my own money in Vanguard funds for the same reasons that I recommend them to others.

Here are the particular Vanguard funds, with fund numbers, that line up with the fund categories I have discussed. These are the funds to ask for when you set up accounts:

Money market fund
Vanguard Prime Money Market Fund (Fund 30)

Index fund
Vanguard Total Stock Market Index Fund (Fund 30)

Bond index fund
Vanguard Total Bond Market Index Fund (Fund 84)

Balanced index fund (60 percent stocks, 40 percent bonds)
Vanguard Balanced Index Fund (Fund 2)

One Additional Suggestion

In my view, Vanguard is the best low-cost fund provider, but some of the people reading this book will find Vanguard's $3,000 account minimum difficult to meet. They would like to get started in investing but don't feel that they can afford to tie up $3,000. After all, you have to keep the account minimum there to keep the account open and in good standing. So you couldn't count on the first $3,000 for your SIT fund (surprises, insurance, taxes).

For these investors, a competitor has emerged to provide lower account minimums: $1,500 to start, or only $50 if you agree to have automatic periodic investments made from a checking account. Here is the name and address of the fund provider:

TIAA-CREF Mutual Funds
P.O. Box 8009
Boston, MA 02266-8009
1-800-223-1200

TIAA-CREF is a well-respected company with a long history and sound management. TIAA-CREF has a fund broadly similar to Vanguard's Total Stock Market Index Fund. It's called the TIAA-CREF Equity Index Fund, and it has the same passive investing strategy but uses a different index to track the overall market. Similarly, the TIAA-CREF Bond Plus Fund works well to offer diversified investments in bonds.

Appendix 2
Checklist—Steps Toward Worry-Free Finances

Now that we've been through your personal finances in detail, here's a handy checklist to help you simplify and improve your finances, one step at a time.

☐ Declare victory and admit defeat. Get the right mental attitude—you're not going to get this perfect, but you're going to do something good, and that's a whole lot better than doing nothing.

☐ Get control of your budget. See where your money is going, if only for a month, and take it from there.

☐ Make sure that you're insured against your major insurable risks. But remember, you don't want to collect.

☐ Make your bank work hard for you. Be sure you don't keep large amounts of money in checking.

☐ Get a roof over your head. Consider what you're spending on shelter, what you're getting and what you should be doing (with attention to what you need, then what you want).

☐ Solve your automotive problems and don't neglect car maintenance. Keep the oil changed and safety items current, if nothing else.

☐ Resolve that you'll start investing early. Buy and hold diversified funds like index funds, even if only a small amount per paycheck.

☐ Don't let your money "leak out" to the tax collector. Also, try not to allow your money to support causes you don't believe in, to the extent this is possible.

☐ Make sure that one of the funds you're investing in is a bond fund. Put more in bonds as you grow older.

☐ Promise yourself that you won't try to "play" the asset markets. Just buy and hold.

☐ Determine the big-ticket items you want to save for, and plan intelligently for them. Don't forget the importance of your time horizon—and play it safe with money needed soon.

☐ Help the children in your life learn about scarcity. They'll never learn if they're given everything.

☐ Prepare your finances, but also your mind and your relationships, for retirement. Go for a smooth transition rather than a big break.

☐ Do your loved ones a huge favor by leaving advance word about medical arrangements and funeral arrangements. If you don't, the rule will be "When in doubt, do more."

☐ Consider your life and your soul. Where are you and what do you need?

Appendix 3
Choosing a Financial Adviser

This book is geared toward helping people make their own decisions without a financial adviser. However, there are times when it can build your confidence and the quality of your decisions to work with a financial adviser.

Unfortunately, the way most financial advisers are paid conflicts directly with the advice of this book. Typically, they get paid a percentage of the money you invest in the funds they offer. Those funds don't include the lowest-cost index funds.

There's nothing dishonest about being paid on commission, and most financial advisers are conscientious about the required disclosures. Still, there's an inherent conflict. They can be paid only if they sell you funds on commission, but the funds that fit best with a long-term buy-and-hold approach don't offer commissions.

All this explains why you need to seek out an adviser offering fee-based financial advice. This adviser will charge you for setting up a financial plan. The charge may be a fixed fee or based on hourly rates, but it won't be a commission for selling particular funds or assets.

If you have the time and discipline to check the qualifications of several financial advisers and interview them extensively, do it. If you don't, ask these questions, carefully noting the answers:

1. Can you work with me on an investment plan that supports

my goals of simplifying my life and honoring God with my finances? (If the answer suggests a lack of respect for your goals or your faith, this isn't the right adviser for you.)

2. What is your opinion of the strategy of buying and holding index funds? (If the answer is something like "It's sound strategy for the long run, though it won't get you spectacular results," fine. If the answer is "I can beat index funds any day," this isn't the right adviser for you.)

3. Can you work with me on a for-fee basis, or do you work on commission only? (You want a for-fee basis. You may be interested in contacting the national association that promotes fee-only planning and maintains a network of fee-only advisers. That's the National Association of Personal Financial Advisors, 355 West Dundee Rd., Suite 200, Buffalo Grove, IL 60089, 1-800-366-2732, or <www.napfa.org>.)

4. What qualifications do you and your company have? (Here you're looking for assurance that the advice will be sound and that your transactions will be handled competently. There are many different groups that certify financial advisers, but that certification does not guarantee the return of any investment. Both good and bad investments are recommended every day by highly credentialed advisers who are trying to beat the market. You can eliminate an important part of the risk by not trying to beat the market.)

What a Financial Adviser Can Do for You

A financial adviser can help you refine your goals and suggest the mix of investment products and services to achieve those goals. The adviser can facilitate the transaction to see that your accounts are set up correctly. The adviser can help you review your progress and your goals periodically to see that your investments are still appropriate. The adviser can also help you avoid unnecessary taxes and keep you posted on changes in the law that may affect you.

What a Financial Adviser Can't Do for You

A financial adviser can't set your goals for you or make you stick with the discipline that it takes to have money to invest. A financial adviser can't guarantee what any particular investment will return, and a good adviser will occasionally remind you of that. A good financial adviser also won't claim an ability to consistently "beat the market" and won't recommend short-term trading strategies that involve frequent transactions. A good financial adviser can't guarantee that your investments will never go down; in fact, for most people the right set of investments will involve occasional losses.

What if you search diligently for fee-based financial advice and can't find it in your community? Or what if you know and trust a financial adviser who works on commission only? You can still get excellent results if you pursue a long-term buy-and-hold, diversified strategy. The returns of this strategy will be high enough to overcome much of the drag caused by commissions and other fees. A good adviser, regardless of fee arrangements, won't make frequent trades or sudden large changes in your portfolio.

One final note: fee-based financial advice won't be cheap. But the services of advisers who work on commission aren't cheap either. If you invest $30,000, 3 percent of that is $900 and 6 percent is $1,800. If that's the size commission you're paying a conventional adviser, that money is paid out of your investment, even though you never write a separate check for it. In fact, one big obstacle to the growth of fee-based financial advice is that commissions keep the fee from being prominent, while a separate fee makes the money that you pay obvious. There are still many investors who think of financial advice as "free" if it comes without a separate bill from someone working on commission.

Therefore, when you find an adviser who will help you buy and hold index funds, don't expect to be advised for free. It will be money well spent if you find the right adviser.

Appendix 4
Notes on Leading Group Study

This book was designed to be easily adapted for individual, group or Sunday school use. Each chapter ends with questions that can be used to structure a session. No previous financial knowledge is required of the group leader; the questions explore attitudes toward money and possessions rather than teaching particular technical financial skills.

What to Keep in Mind as a Group Leader

1. Arrange for the meeting place and make sure it is comfortable before participants arrive. You will need a flip chart, blackboard or overhead projector for some questions.

2. Look over the chapter you will be discussing. Pay particular attention to any necessary preparation (for example, cards or pieces of paper). Much of your work as a leader will involve collecting responses from group members, sharing them with the group and leading the discussion that follows. People are usually willing to discuss the subject matter if they are given a little encouragement.

3. Sample answers to the discussion questions are posted online at <www.plainmoney.com>.

4. At the beginning of each session, welcome participants and

briefly summarize the chapter being discussed. Then work through the group discussion questions. Typically, answering the questions and discussing the responses will take 45-60 minutes.

5. Five minutes before your scheduled ending time, wrap up discussion and find out if there are unanswered questions. Ask for volunteers to research the questions and report to the group at the next session.

6. Give some thought to the role of prayer in your sessions. Some groups will want to open and close with prayer; some will want to share their financial struggles with each other; others will want to keep their financial struggles entirely to themselves. Make sure that the group understands that conversations about financial struggles should be kept in confidence, not shared outside the group.

You can cover this book in one Sunday school quarter by discussing one chapter each week. Experience suggests that the pace is quite feasible. A four-session study should include chapters one and six through nine, with chapters one and six covered together in a single (busy) first session and the remaining chapters treated weekly.

Index